T0329433

Language, Thought, Art & Existence:
Creative Nonfictions

Tendai R. Mwanaka

Langaa Research & Publishing CIG
Mankon, Bamenda

Publisher
Langaa RPCIG
Langaa Research & Publishing Common Initiative Group
P.O. Box 902 Mankon
Bamenda
North West Region
Cameroon
Langaagrp@gmail.com
www.langaa-rpcig.net

Distributed in and outside N. America by African Books Collective
orders@africanbookscollective.com
www.africanbookscollective.com

ISBN-10: 9956-762-10-5

ISBN-13: 978-9956-762-10-1

© Tendai R. Mwanaka 2017

Table of Contents

Introduction... v

1. Language, Thought and Reality.....................1

2. The Writer's Experience........................... 11

3. Memories and Memoir Writing.....................23

4. The Caine Workshop and African
writing reflections: How I decided
on "Notes from Mai Mujuru's breast"...............27

5. My Volmoed Journey...............................45

6. Nyanga, December 2015:
In Search of Ancient Ways.........................61

7. Collectivism vs. Individualism.................... 73

8. Desire and Pasion................................. 77

9. Death (Life)...................................... 83

10. Doubt.. 89

11. Dear John.. 95

12. It's Not About Me: Dairies (2010-2011).......... 103

13. Age Has No Numbers………….…………. 121

14. Gathering Evidence:
Dairies (2012-2013) ……………..………………. 133

15. Running Away From the Lotus Position…….. 157

16. The Evidence of Things Said:
Dairies (2014-2015) …………………………..………163

17. Coldplay's X&Y, Angels, Him and Her……… 175

18. A Date with Jonathon Matimba:
An Appreciation of the Legendary
Zimbabwean Sculptor………………………..………. 189

19. Music and Me…………….………………… 201

References…………………………………….……207

Introduction

Language, Thought, Art and Existence comprises 19 critical and personal essays, written in a creative way that centres around the topics of language, thought, art and existence. Instead of writing highly critical scholarly essays that one would expect with the title, this collection continues with my ideology of presenting non-fiction in a creative, fresh, easy to read, simple language, with most of the essays driven by personal stories, thus making it accessible to a wide spectrum of readers from the scholarly (academic) to journalistic to general readers. I grouped the pieces according to the topics, with the language and writing essays starting the book.

I started with Language essays as I feel for us to communicate we need a language first, and in these language essays I tried to define the parameters of what I will discuss in the book. The first language essay entitled *Language, Thought and Reality* bends to the academic scholastic genre as it deals with what is language, how language is constructed by the people and the world, and inversely how language defines the people and the world, how thoughts are part of the language of a people, and how all these are shaped by the reality in which they happen. The second essay, *The Writer's Experience*, is on writing and the language I create with my writing, what inspires me, what am I trying to attempt with my writing. It is still a look at language but from the writer's perspective. The third essay is on memory and memoir writing, entitled *Memories and Memoir Writing,* in which I investigate the neural paths of memories, how to extract memories to create memoirs. How memoir writing gives us a perspective seat to come to terms with who we were, who we are now, who we want to be in the future. The fourth essay deals with the writing process as writer. I didn't want to throw abstract theories on my writing process, so I used the personal route, in which I explored how I got to write the story, *Notes From Mai Mujuru's Breast*, a story I wrote for the 2012 Caine Prize Anthology. Thus the essay is entitled *The Caine Workshop and African writing reflections: How I decided on "Notes from Mai Mujuru's breast"*. Not only do I explore the writing, but the Caine workshop idea, how it works to write a story under workshop conditions, and it also gives perspectives into the African writing landscape. The essay is written in a funny, jocular, explorative way. Whilst this is one way in which I get to write I didn't proffer it as the only way I get to write, as I will later explore several other ways in the book, especially in the three diary series. Whilst the 4 essays on language and writing I have outlined are not comprehensive, they give a clear path to delineate my ideas and thoughts around Language and writing, which I continuously explored in the coming topics.

The language essays are followed by travel and thought essays. I do think a lot when I am walking or travelling, thus I have realised this is one of the best ways to process thought, through travel. Using the concepts I have highlighted in the previous section of language, I open out my thoughts in this group of essays. The first travel essay, *My Volmoed Journey,* is on my travel process to the Caine workshop in Volmoed, South Africa, the travels we did around Volmoed, the travels that were happening inside me during the 10 days' workshop. I tried to juxtapose the two travel routes, the one inside me, and the one physical, and also the historical aspects of the Volmoed and its environs. The second essay is on my travel back to where I came from, Nyanga Zimbabwe, which I did in December 2015, entitled *Nyanga, December 2015: In Search of*

Ancient Ways. In this travel essay I strike a strong parallel with a historical issue that I am interested in, that is exploring ancient ways that were there before my civilisation in this area. As I noted in the memoir writing essay, there is no *now* without the *past.* There is no *future* without the *past,* thus in this travel piece I tried to shed connections between the past and the future, through the present. The next essay is *Collectivism vs Individualism.* I think the world over they have been discussions around these issues in several ways like the 99 percent versus the 1 percentage discussions, protests, movements we saw a few years ago. These I felt could be explored on a binary line between Collectivism Vs Individualism. I explore the pros and cons of both outlooks, and tried to bridge them, in trying to find the best way forward as humanity. The next 3 thought essays form the core of my thought root and drives it, that is Death *(Death(Birth)),* Desire *(Desire and Passion)* and Doubt *(Doubt).* I feel the tripod of life, being, existence rests on these legs (tripods). Death conditions us in this life, makes us realise our existence is tenuous in this state, gives us the time parameter to shape ourselves. Desire fires our lives, imaginations, ambitions. It sweetens or not, our lives. Doubt gives us the questions to find answers, to as who we are, to our existential dilemmas. I tried to explore each of the three, academically, philosophical, psychologically and personally, with personal stories grounding the discussion into what is real and believable. The last thought essay looks at one issue that seems to be at the centre of humanity's deepest obsession, SEX. But instead of writing dos and don'ts, or instead of writing religious, philosophical, scholarly constructions of this issue, I decided on personalising it, and write it as part story, part essay, part humour. It is a funny take at sex as I used other worlds than that of the human to try to unbundle this obsession with sex that we now have. The essay is simply entitled *Dear John*.

These thought essays are followed by existential essays. In this group of essays I focussed on me, the writer, the person. In this group the diary drive the essays, with 3 diary periods between 2010 up to 2015 *(It's Not about Me: Dairies (2010-2011), Gathering Evidence: Dairies (2012-2013) The Evidence of Things Said: Dairies (2014-2015))*. I just recorded what was happening around me, in me around that time, in Zimbabwe, in Chitungwiza. But I also dealt with several issues like the political situation in Zimbabwe, music, reading, writing, language, thoughts, spiritual, etc. The other essays that breaks these dairies are personal too, one dealing with a breaking down relationship, *Age Has No Numbers*, one on life changes, *Running Away From The Lotus Position*.

The next and last group of essays are on art. As I have already noted I avoided writing abstract essays on art but used several personal routes to explore what art is. The first art essay is entitled Coldplay's *X&Y, Angels, Him and Her*. I love this band's music thus I show in this essay how listening to this band's music, especially on this album helped me deal with that dying relationship that I have highlighted in the existential essays above. But it's not just personal. It's how that music could be used by others to deal with their existential dilemmas too, but goes further in exploring the music and art of the Coldplay as a band, as an artist, as a phenomena, as an institution. The second art essay looks at the first individual I knew on a personal level who was an artist, his life, his artistic call, our relationship, how that might have helped instil this love of art I have. The essay is entitled *A Date with Jonathon Matimba: An Appreciation of the Legendary Zimbabwean Sculptor*. Through exploring the visual artworks and life of my uncle,

Jonathon Matimba, I also explore what I might sometimes be trying to attempt with my visual art, that of being the storyteller. The last art essay is entitled *Music and Me*, and these two M(s) are very important to me now. Music and Me. I love music. In this essay I am not singing, I am not making music, I am not doing music notes, no. I am just exploring all that as a listener of music. I love listening to music; this is where my greater talent lies- listening.

Thus throughout the book, as the new adage the *personal is political*, I let this *personal* drive these essays as I tried to investigate what I thought was language, existence and art. This book is invaluable to the academic establishment, social theorists, linguists, literary theorists, activists and the general readers.

Language, Thought and Reality

In, *The Foundations of Language: Talking and reading to young children. Andrew Wilkinson, 1971* defines Language as "primarily a system of agreed sounds and these sounds stands for or symbolises objects, process and relationships." A good example of these sounds is word. Words can also be symbolised by combinations of letters. Linguists differentiate between instinctive noises like grunts, a cry of pain, and non-instinctive noises. They say instinctive sounds are not part of language. They agree that non instinctive sounds are part of language. I have a bone to pick up with these linguists. As a literature practitioner, I protest. I think both non instinctive and instinctive sounds should make up language; after all these instinctive sounds, like a cry of pain, differ with languages and language groups. Instinctive sounds in the language they are created make up that language, and there are agreed to upon by the users of that language to mean something. Some of these instinctive sounds, even though they started as instinctive sounds sometimes end up being non instinctive sounds, still expressing an instinctive feeling. For instance in my Shona language and culture if someone is crying they mostly call out *Maiwe...eee*, which is a word, used when calling your mother to help you, even *hi,hi,hi...* can mean more than the crying sound that it is usually associated with. To a poet, the wind, the water, the mountains..., have their own languages that are instinctive.

Thought is, "the formation and arrangement of ideas" *Catherine Soanes (ed), Sara Hawker (ed) and Julia Elliott (ed), Paperback Oxford English Dictionary, 2001.* In our minds, there are images and symbols of real things and unreal things and there is no need for words. When we think about these things we think in pictures. The thought like the one described above usually, but not always, occur in animals, or in dreams. The thought here is in its symbolic quality character or as often referred to; it is "internalised imitation." It is when the mind imitates objects happening outside it. As noted above this thought doesn't require language for it to occur. It requires pictures, which though in another sense is a type of language on its own. There is also thought brought on when the mind grapples with or imitate things inside itself, not images outside it. There are images we have stored inside our minds, what we might call memories. For us to bring memories out we have to imitate (recall) them for us to think about them.

Another way to represent events and things is through words. Words can also be used to create or bring to the fore images, to create pictures, even colours like a painter. Thus, "a symbolic function, therefore exist which is broader than language that both encompass both the system of verbal signs and that of symbolic (picture)" Paiget, J (1968). The symbolic function is the source of thought. Thought then can be defined as the capacity to symbolise things (to oneself or others) and it precedes language. Language though has a pervading influence on thought. It transforms thought by helping it to attain its forms of balance by means of (more) advanced schematisation and a more mobile abstraction. That's why people who are deaf have a handicap, because they mostly think with little or no language. Language can be used less picturesquely, but in much more exact, economically way through abstraction and generalisation. These are language's two qualities that can be used to express thought. There is also language that is complex, poetical, or picturesque, that requires definition

2

(understanding) through more words, through maybe paraphrasing.

"Concept formation" is how easily we could navigate through language to describe our thoughts so that they would become accessible. "Concept is an abstraction from objects, situations, or events of the attributes these phenomena have in common...", *E Stones (1966)*, in his book, *An Introduction to Educational Psychology* explore the words we sometimes use to symbolise or stand for these concepts. He says the idea of tree is a concept, or even that of animals, education, writing.... They all refer to a class of things, situations, events, or objects, not just one thing. From multitudes of different types of animals, Lions, hyenas, dogs..., we abstract the essential similarities and ignore the inessential differences. So we call them animals, which is a generic term. It doesn't refer to one animal in particular, but all such things in general. We could explore it further and say lions are a concept for they are different types of lions. Words like animals or lions stimulate generalisation. The possession of concepts is so much part of our thinking. They provide us with an "advanced schematisation". Try to visualise a situation whereby there is a world in which concepts are not a part of our thinking. It's untenable, for you can't even start. Advanced schematisation is a classificatory system by which we are able to relate to experiences one to another. Tomatoes or a tomato is wrongly thought of as a vegetable, especially when combined with other vegetables, in meat or in many other dishes. That's what we generally think. But, a tomato is rather a fruit, of the family of citric fruits. This could be as far as we could go to identify this fascinating fruit. It's difficult to recognise it as a vegetable, much less as a fruit.

Concepts store our experiences, more so they cut away details to enable us to see essentials. Now we know a tomato is a fruit, rather than generally as a vegetable. Concept acquisition through language is essential for our thinking beyond the elemental level. It is important to note that concepts are manmade, that they do not exist in nature and the good examples of this are concepts related to existence (how do you know that you exist, what is existence, who are you), concepts related to time, space and direction (the question is on how, or where you start from, what you start with, to which direction). Exploring the time concept: why should there be 60 seconds in a minute, 60 minutes in an hour, and 24 hours in a day? The whole point is man decided to divide time in that way. Had he decided to divide it differently we might have 120 seconds in a minute, and the resulting differences in terms of minutes in an hour, and hours in a day. Some clever industrialists in Britain would do that, changing the clock to run very slowly during working hours and very fast during lunch hour such that workers would clock more hours in a day. It is all about what we think is important that create these concepts and then they are passed down as truths by humanity. It is this way man creates the world in which he lives by means of a language. It is this way man creates his own reality.

Man moves through in this construction of reality the way children moves from a situation in which their initial universe is entirely centred in his/her own body and his actions are egocentrism (unconscious). A child after 18 months begins a general decentring process. Linguists call it the Copernican revolution. It is when Copernicus, in his Copernican revolution (7th century), discovered, rather that the planets circles around the sun, not as previously thought around the earth. At 18 months the child begins to regard himself as an object among many others in a universe made up of permanent objects, in which there is at work a causality that is both localised in space and objectified in things. Construction of reality can then be loosely defined as how we built up concepts from objects, situations and events and from other concepts. We internalise, that is, making a part of our own thinking the ways of thought, the view of our elders. The reality (the views of our elders) is manmade. The question is how far this reality does (manmade) correspond to the reality outside. And, as the Copernican revolution posits: as we grow older we come to think the world doesn't revolve around us, thus our thinking becomes less egocentric. We make interpretations according to the information we have, fitted into the inner schematisation we have so far developed at some stages earlier.

A child at six years old asks why a marble is rolling downhill, and is told that it is on an incline. He is not satisfied with this explanation and says "it knows someone is down there who is calling for it to come downhill," *Wilkinson, 1971*. This is animism, whereby inanimate objects are endowed with human characteristics, just as his nursery toys are. At that stage the boy has developed to the stage where he understands something of human motive but not of physical principles.

The above explanation can only apply in realties that believe physical objects don't have human characterises. There are Indian (American), and African worlds that still believes in the reality of physical objects having a human, symbolic, or even spiritual characteristics. In Nyanga, Zimbabwe, where I grew up, physical objects like mountains, pools, stones, animals such as the python, lion, and the white baboon are believed to have human and or superhuman characteristics and are believed to be the owners of the area, not the people.

This reality is quite different from the Global North reality. This reality, even the young children's reality is fascinating for writers and poets (William Black's "songs of innocence", and "songs of experience" is one example of this fascination), not because it represents Eden, but it is the freshness of it, without schematisation that enthrals the writers.

It makes me recall an episode in the Ally Mcbeal Soap where there is this child who is suffering from an advanced form of leukaemia, and is facing death any moment. The medicine is unbelievably too expensive for the family to afford. They have approached their church for help but were denied any funding. Ally Mcbeal, acted by Calista Flockhart, a lawyer, visits the child whilst she is visiting her boyfriend who is the doctor of this child. She is with her friend, Lucy Liu, who is a retired Stanford law graduate. When the child hears the two are lawyers he asks that they help him in filing a lawsuit against God. It is unthinkable to our adult reality, but to this child it is. God is responsible for the cancer. God (through the church) should have paid for the medicine so the child holds God responsible and accountable.

In the above two stories of children; the children stood outside received opinion, and threw up the ambiguity of their mother's languages. The freedom of children from accepted opinions results in unconscious insight that cut at the very fabric of society. To William Black, construction of reality is the progress of innocence into experience. The human brain is the source of the world of experience. We live in the world our brain creates. This world is not however, necessarily evil. The Black's tiger, breaking out of the "forest of the night" is a symbol of the richer, fuller, more imaginative life man can create. In one sense we are always in the same position as the children above. Their limited schematisation gave them a

6

limited view of reality. Ours is less limited and gives us a wider notion of reality, but it is still limited. The language we use has considerable effect on our view of reality, and on our consequent behaviours.

Benjamin, Lee Whorf (1966), in his book *Language, Thought and Reality*, on *The relation of habitual thought and behaviour to our language*, formulated the theories known as the Whorfian hypothesis. He acknowledged his debt to *Edward Sapir (1921), Language: An Introduction to Study of Speech*. Sapir thus posits,

> Human beings do not live in an objectified world alone, nor alone in a world of social activity as ordinarily understood, but are very much at the mercy of the particular language which has become the medium of expression for their society. It is quite an illusion to imagine that one adjust to reality essentially without the use of language and the language is merely an incidental means of solving specific problems of communication and reflection. The fact of the matter is that the "real world" is to a larger extent unconsciously built up on the language habits of the group... We see and hear and otherwise experience very largely as we do because the language habits of our community predispose certain choices of interpretations.

William Black said "a fool sees not the same tree as a wise man sees". Whorf could have paraphrased it differently "A San, or Taureg sees not the same sand dune as say an Englishman", or that "a Yupik, or Inuit sees not the same snow as say an Englishman." For the San and the Yupik, Whorf pointed out that the class "snow" or say "sand dune" in English would seem too general to them. There have different words for mobile, wind moving, falling, drifting, stationary, dormant sand dunes or snow. In contrast the Aztecs (Hopi language) of the American Indians has one word for ice, snow and cold, one noun that covers everything that flies with the exception of birds. Insects, aviators, airplanes are known by the same noun.

In Shona language, the Manicaland dialect has different words for sweet potatoes and the seeds (Madima and Rubvanda, respectively), but in the Mashonaland dialect (Zezuru), they are referred to using the same word or variations of (Mbambaira). So if you say Rubvanda to someone from Mashonaland they wouldn't understand you. The problem is not that certain things can be said in one language and not in another language, but it rather is how easily and habitually are they said. For these will determine the tendency of thought. The word "conscience" in French should stand for "consciousness" and in English "conscience" indicates a more fundamental difference in thinking.

Whorf studied North American Indian languages such as Hopi and found the grammatical organisation to be different from that of most Standard Average European (S.A.E) languages. This different organisation implied a different view of reality. In SAE there are nouns and verbs, things and actions. The nouns "exist", long term and the verbs are what happen to nouns, in the short term. Whorf asks if: "strike, turn, run," are verbs, because they refer to short lasting events and actions, why is "fist" a noun? Why are "lighting, spark, wave, pulsation, storm, spasms, emotions etc.," nouns in contrast to why are "keep, adhere, project, dwell, persist", verbs? Then there is the long lasting phenomenon like "house" and "man". Whorf is pointing out there are means of classifications different from the ones we employ in Hopi language, where "lighting, flame, pulsation." are verbs. Hopi has actually a classification of events (linguistic isolates) by duration type, something that is strange to our modes of thought. The biggest import of this essay then and of Whorf's hypothesis is on the way language habitually channels our thoughts. In order to sum up Whorf's hypothesis and the essay we will conclude with his actual words.

We are thus introduced to a new principle of relativity which holds that all observers are not led by the same physical evidence to the same picture of the universe, unless their linguistic backgrounds are similar or can in some way be calibrated... That modern Chinese or Turkish scientist describe the world in the same terms as Western scientists describe means, of course, only that they have taken over the entire Western system of rationalisations, not that they have corroborated that system from their native powers of observation. *Benjamin, Lee Whorf (1966)*

The Writer's Experience

When writing I want to mix different forms, formats, styles, genres, moulding all these into a writing that will stand on its own, for itself. I do away with, in fact I don't think about what kind of style, format, genre I have to be faithful to. I play on the boundaries. I try to stretch the limits. I do away with the "taught" five paragraphs approach to essay writing and go for writing that simply say something that confounds, that mean something. I take discrete traits of writing (ideas, content, organisation, voice, word choice, sentence fluency and conventions) as negative reinforcements so I don't think of them (I am unaware of them) as I do my writing. I let go off internalised story scripts and negatively reinforced simplifications by accessing the other alternatives to fill the void.

It's a void inside me that propels me to write, like we seek food, love, appreciation, to quench different types of hungers and wants in us. I have to write to sooth or quench this void. I use those reinforced simplifications noted above to reach the real "me" inside me. This inner "me" is what makes up that void inside me that makes me want to write so as to sooth it or quench it off, and like hunger, once I have quenched it, I feel real good with myself, but it comes back again and like hunger I have to write some more to quench it again. So, it becomes an endless or perpetual process of hunger and feedings. That's why I feel I don't know how to stop doing this, or being part of this. If I can't write it's as if I have forgotten to breath.

In doing my writing, I shed away generalisations and opinions of me (I hate to be read as necessarily a black writer, or an African writer, or even "other" writer. Being logged into these boxes, you are forced to think or write according to these boxes' constructs), by adapting my internalised subjective "me" scripts, or even conversely revising these conditioned "me" narratives through grappling with the complexities of the "me" story. So, my writing acts as an ability to actively challenge, disrupt, and overturn generationally internalised oppression.

The language that I use is of paramount importance. I always write in a language close to my dialect. I believe there is a very rich Zimbabwean form of English that has evolved for over a century now. An American writer needs American tools, bends the language towards his environment and experience, like for instance, American music, sports, life, even wars like the Vietnam and Iraq wars influences his writing. He doesn't have to rely on the British experience, culture and environment but his own. This creates a new language. As an African writer I mix English, my mother tongue (Shona), any other mediums of communication I have come into contact with, my experience, culture and geographical perspective to fashion my unique writing and language. Wole Soyinka, Sembene Ousmane, Ngugi Wa Thiong'o fashioned out their works using their language experience and cultures. Their works are different from each other, let alone from that of say, Salman Rushdie who uses his British-Indian experience in his work.

When I am writing the subconscious (the "me" story) comes on top and becomes the agent of speech, action, thought and narration. This subconscious "me" is built up of my culture, geographic perspective, language and beliefs, and my innate personality. This innate personality takes over all these and it is the agent of the writing. I write about what my senses have brought inside me (that which is mostly in my world's view of things, that which comprise of my thoughts, feelings and emotions, deep inside of me) such that the language resultant is a language in itself. It is the qualities of its intrinsicalities that should confound. Though, as I have noted above, I write in English, this intrinsic English language is affected by my everyday life, language, the language associated with my thoughts, emotions and feelings. Sometimes it will be a language of images. I have to find words (verbal) to represent, very closely, this language of images in which the thinking, or image conception or making, or beginnings of the writing have occurred.

There are critics who would want to make us believe there are rigid rules to creativity. That a writer should write like this and that way is wrong, and usually it's the Global North world's perspective we are forced to gulp. My thinking is that rules of writing tend to be exorable, that they should change, and that if they are applied rigidly (using a single world's view) they become stumbling blocks to the writer. Modernist writers and poets (Pound, Elliot, Yeats, and Joyce) had to mock the contained novel and poetry form of the 18th century, so did before these, the metaphysical poets to the Elizabethan (17th century) conventions to our great benefit. The beat generation mocked and problematized American oppressive societies of the fifties and sixties, and the off-beat outlook helped to develop the beat's thinking but in an off-beat (anti-beat) way. In all these movements and many others there was a constant need to change, to confront their realties, to find new ways of thinking, feeling, being, to be explorers when writing, thus to create writing as an innovation of the possibility of language.

Listening to *Charles Bernstein and Bruce Andrews* talking about *Language* with *Susan Howe, Pacifica Radio in the 1979*, I find what I want to believe I am also I attempting to do when I am writing. Bruce Andrews says he goes "back to all these traditions in literature, to dibble with questions that have been dominant in other advanced arts, to philosophy..." To questions raised by the philosophers as to what is language, thinking, living, being, existence, to politics, music, art, to all these as confluences. I also go back to all these but my biggest source is from writers, thinkers, artists who are working and living now, writers whom I inhabit the same time and space with. I illuminate, and collaborate with these writings, especially that which is being written now. All these creates the media in which my writing happens, which is language.

Charles Bernstein, in the interview, feels this language is not "some concocted version brought to us by the critical establishment." I also feel rules-governed creativity (usually of the critical establishment) can only result in writing that is constrained, an achievement that is passionless, and "this insistence that language should be clear, on opacity, exhaust the limits of our interest and dialogue and represses knowledge, *Bernstein* says and continues with the dialogue and says "this insistence on this minor tradition (straight-jacketed) in literature results in conservative interpretations of the world." He says it lies in the sensibilities of people who teach English at academic institutions and that this view is the one they try to push on society and society generally wants to consume things so it is seduced to buy into this conception of reality as the truth, but the real truth is that "we create our own world through language."

Our language develops from respecting the other different worlds from ours out there and different conceptions out there. Language should be a system and it has to shape writing and the people, and the writing and people shape the language in return. It means when we create language we create ourselves. The world is constructed through language. For example, Bruce Andrews says his political writing looks at how values are constituted, how labour is always removed as part of production. This way of looking at social phenomena (politics) contrary to the above, is always limiting. It should be about participatory not of acceptance. Its people who make up the language, or any social phenomena and the social phenomena (language, politics) should be the vessel in which people work in, not itself becoming the centre of meaning. It means it should change with the people.

Bruce Andrews says when social phenomena (language) become the centre of meaning it limits the system. One would become encouraged to take things for granted. It can also be used as a source of social control by a small percentage of the society (language in its imperialistic sense), and between individuals, between activities etc. Bernstein and Andrews agrees that Language should be used to practise and problematizing the system. It should be the means of production. Language should create the world, and things that stand on their own. It should be fluid, non-instrumental. Language should not be an act of transcription of a pre-constituted and pre-conceived world. Language should not be an apparatus of social control.

Like Bernstein and Andrews I don't want to eliminate any idiosyncrasies. *Rachel Blau DuPlessis* speaking at the *Tyler school of Art, Philadelphia (1985)* with *Clark Coolidge, Michael palmer, John Yau and Geoffrey Young*, and the topic is on *image, imaging part 2*, says she experiments with typos, ungramaticalness; for uniformity to her kills the language. I resonate with this and I am not saying as a writer I do not want to work within some rule-framework but rather that the writer should be allowed to make concessions and conscious rules and decisions, rules that apply to the world the writer is writing from.

I find a straightforward, logical kind of writing whereby for stories, one action leads to another logically, until the story gradually develops and culminates into a climax as limiting and unexciting. In the introduction note to the novel *The Black Insider* by *Dumbudzo Marechera, Flora Veit-Wild* says Marechera felt a straight forward novel was oppressive and would freeze thoughts and thought patterns. The reader already knows how the story will pan out after a couple or so paragraphs or passages so that many a reader would feel discouraged from exploring the story because already the reader has conquered its scope. "It's like exploring an old stream with a new boat." *I am now Bulletproof*, in *Keys in the River, Tendai Mwanaka 2012*. One is bound to skim or skip over the middle passages and rush to the conclusion. Most of the novels in the Heinemann African Writer's Series follows this, so also genre fictions like romantic novels, spy novels etc. You always know the bad guy will get his comeuppance, the good will always succeed, the hero will succeed, have overwhelming glory and respect, find love and happily lives ever after. These works were fashioned out along the Bible's parables. There is no world, or very little of it for the plot, and the climax to take another twist, a turn, to confound, to challenge the reader.

It's sick to still hear that writers have to write novels that don't ask for more from the readers. This portrayal of readers as stupid human beings by the critical establishment is unfair. There are very intelligent, up to date, and complex readers out there who don't benefit from this kind of patronising by the critical establishment. My writing has shifting points of view, in space and time. My writing has multiplicity of narrative voices (there is always a story, even in essays, a narration), a narration-within-a-narration, multiple crises and climaxes, surprises, delayed information, leaps, reversals, free stream of consciousness, deliberate confusion, the playing against image, image making and sound, against grammaticalness, breaking up of the textiness of the text. I have to move from reality to fantasy and imaginations back to reality without the limits of time and space. I can write stories that are documentaries, or poetry, or even essays. I can write essays that are poetry, or diary, or anything else. I can write drama that is anti-drama... I can write poetry that is chunks of philosophical discourse or reasoning. My writing is always about philosophy.

Bernadette Mayer in the article, *Secret passageways/Nathaniel Hawthorne vs Bernadette Mayer* by *J Morris* in *Eleven Eleven Journal, issue 9, 2010*, feels philosophy is always at stake in her writing. Ideas, the frame-tale of allegory, she grants these ideas a primacy in her writing. To me these are allegories that are self-referential but not always. It is about the confusion between writing, living and being, thus I compose all my writing from days lived as an individual, a nation, or even the entire globe. But it is always with a twist. The life of the mind is the source and its quarry in the writing that assumes. Ideas, allegories, philosophy is the source of the writing and its quarry. Morris feels that all the theories that fires up the mind towards writing are important, for they are "the hidden struts and beams of a house, inside of which the writing happens." Like Bernadette Mayer, I am always on the darker, more stylistically subversive, with forms mutating. Each of my writing mutates into something different from the other writings. There is the omniscience narrator, drama, soap opera, comic, satirical, the diary, reportage, poetical, scholarly, fantasy, autobiographical,

biographical, third person narrator, letter, cutting up things, juxtaposing images and a direct author's intervention to take over the character's role. What matters is the quality of the world it creates. Like Marechera, but on a circumspect level, most of my characters are a variant of me, the author-narrator. I don't always develop one character at the detriment of the other characters, one point of view at the detriment of others that require illuminating, one perspective, so also one type of writing. I despair of one character, one perspective, one thinking. It should be about the totality of these that matters. My biggest hero (thinking, perspective) is always the people. The people I interact with each and every day, people who are reading my work, the person in me. I am deeply connected and sympathetic to my characters, especially public reaction to their moral choices. This inclusivity of contrastive characters, images, thinking, beliefs and even writing creates writing that is scopic, complex and confounding. But a reader who is prepared to follow me along paths of thoughts, consciousness, imaginations, fantasies, realties and memories will duly be rewarded.

There are instances as a writer when you have an obligation to your readers to suggest solutions and interpretations especially when the writing deals with abstract philosophical issues. The biggest job when doing that is not to force your readers to accept or agree with your suggested interpretations. Most of the times you just have to let your readers come to their own conclusions and your job is to open a whole arena in which the readers can enjoy your work and come to their own conclusions. I always encourage them to agree or disagree with me, to take whatever path they deem correct, to recreate my work whilst they are reading it. Readers, in fact when I am a reader, I don't want to be a tourist (a tourist comes to consume things, to enjoy tourist attractive things, to leave without giving something back, carrying only the image of the thing and leaving everything behind). A tourist work from the outside and stays outside. I am saying tourists don't enter the Victoria Falls, but enjoy it from the outside, in a safe distance and space. Rather I want my readers to be pilgrims, to undergo a pilgrimage of some sort, to enter their own Mecca. They should be participants. The writing should affect them and they should affect the writing. They should be reading my work and as well creating more work out of what I have written, or what I have left undeveloped, or unwritten. Good writing, at most, should generate more writing. This symbiotic relationship is a complete equation in itself.

Another important area I am constantly exploring is on motivation. I like to think there are some behaviours that don't necessarily comes from a motive, or maybe it's impossible, without some psycho-analysis tools, to unearth the motivation or explanations behind them. Sometimes I work from these misguided assumptions. Another equally contentious issue is of showing or telling the story. There is always the critic's exhortation that a writer should not tell, but show the story. I sometimes work against this as well. Critics want to tell the author that he has to achieve balance on dialogue, action, thought and narration in a story as if more of one of these would render the work less powerful. This insistence on a calibrated balance is untenable. I don't want to think everything can be broken down into pieces, be put on a magnifying glass and have rationality applied to it. In fact, I am refractory to rationality. I think in images, metaphors, institutions, like woman usually do. There are people, or things, or even behaviours that don't ask for rationality. There are whole in their complexity, their unexplainability.

Content is another bow in the arrow of my writing. I always want to be relevant to someone out there. I always include a lot of content matter in my work. It is the most important aspect of any writing. Whilst I think being aware of language is important, I think it is more important when you are saying something. I think form and style, that critics usually concentrate on, is not as important as content. My writing circles around issues of relativity of human existence, issues of subjectivity to perception, function and substance of a person in relation to the human and physical background surrounding him.

My writing circle around the need to confront issues of struggle and conflicts, whether individual, community, nation, global, social, political, religious or spiritual etc... My writing circles around issues of alienation and identity searching, especially in the context of founding and building of relationships and the drive toward satisfaction and happiness. My writing is an act of reproduction like giving birth. Pregnancy is like over-expressiveness in writing. This want to write, this want in us to reproduce (too much), this over-expressiveness, the resistance to it, within it, in it, is the complications of my writing. I write to resist this (over-expressiveness), not to give up, to change the language.

I work within the every day. Morris quotes Emerson calling them "the days themselves are gods." in his poem "Days." It is days that deal with issues of relationships, love, alienation and its attendant pathos and banality- loss, loneliness, death. It is days that deal with social and political issues, religious and spiritual issues. It's Whalen's "a graph of mind moving" that I create, or what Morris calls "a massive-hot-house of ideas," or William Blake's "weird interconnected boiler rooms of thoughts." My characters or I myself confront these issues straightforward, in a frank, sincere and honest way. I stand by what I believe in, what I think, what I see. I want to strip-naked all attitudes and attitudinizing, human or otherwise, to expose the naked brutality of our societies like the Beat writers, to unmask the violence we perpetrate against each other, and get to the core of things.

If we can come to grips with things, if we can see issues for what they are, we will start the healing process. You do not heal by covering the wound but rather by exposing it to the elements and find a way out. It's about trying to find a way forward. It is about hope, a ray of warning light in a dark tunnel. It is about trying to reach that light and thus freeing one's self from the darkness. My writing is about being healed, you and me, the author the reader. It is a no-holds barred pursuit of the truth.

3

Memories and Memoir Writing

Memories are a fragmented thing, a living thing, living deep inside us. They are subjected to the neural paths created by information later discovered, and proximity to the recollections. Some of the information discovered could be through fragment stories, photographs, people, the environment, speech, etc... These would invoke a person to recollect about the memory that they associate with the above prompters. But for the person to invoke the memory they have to still be closer to it. In writing memoirs, I have discovered that it is difficult to memorise about my early life memories, especially those that happened to me when I was still less than five years old. I don't remember a lot of stuff from that time, so for me to try to write about that period, I feel I misremember some chunks of it.

In the essay *Mother's Body* in *Zimbabwe: The Blame Game* I wrote, "The childhood home becomes immemorial and recollected time. Memories and imaginations shape it", thus, I have always thought most memoirs are partly factious, partly nonfiction. The fiction doesn't only come in when we are writing about the memoirs, or recollecting about them, but it's a process that starts from when we log the events or memories into our psyche. Our minds creates this a-bit-reality and a-bit-factious world, in logging these events, and over the years, it continuously recreates them, like we are always rewriting history, thus by the time we record the memoirs, there is a lot of fiction in them. Even in those memories that we still remember easily, we invent to make them into coherent narration. It means when we are trying to remember things we will be misremembering things because of distance to experience.

"I don't find enough blood or flesh in these memories but fragments of faded memories and, more dancing shadows the more I have stayed away from home." I wrote in *Mother's Body*, an essay on exile, writing about distance created by the exilic condition. The memories becomes like a home we would love to return to, we feel we can only find ourselves if we were to make that journey back into this home. It's like the same feeling those living in exile would have about their originating home.

The beauty of memoir writing or recollection is that it creates several narrative paths or strands. Memoir writing or recollection doesn't follow a linear seeming narrative path; its form should be like bubbles in a pool, thus it comes from all over the landscape. It would be like a child learning to talk for the first time. The stage feminist French critic, Helen Cixious calls semiotic babbling stage. You need to exercise balance, somehow, in the writing so that someone reading it can be able to follow you, thus there is a lot of re-writing, recollecting, revising, in trying to structure this babbling semiotic world. Thus, there should be a good grasp of techniques of recalling emotions, accessing emotions, shaping scenes from experience, and developing characters.

The bubbles could be bubbles of thought, of dialogue, of events, of illustrations, of varying scales of lives. All these imitate the cyclical nature of thinking and the associative paths we delineate for ourselves. The mind always scans its files for connections and patterns. In doing this it encounters what it has stored, or recreated over the years, thus there is a layering that happens. I would like to think this happens the way

Istanbul was layered into different layers of architecture, depicting civilisations that have inhabited the city; each layer being made to sit on top of the other layer. It takes the very best of memoir writers to imbue these layers in their memoir writing.

When the memory is thus layered, the humans define some sort of order out of a maelstrom of memory, like a kind of translucent lens, looking at both the physical and the emotional.

Memoir writing or recollection is a means of using textual, verbal or graphical language to narrate autobiographies or memories, to discover the aspects of our pasts, and to express hope for the future. It allows us an opportunity to pause and to take a vantage point from which to explore the inner and outer landscape. These pauses are enormous moments for all of us and thus they allow us to ask ourselves whether we are proud of the people we have become. *What did we do wrong or right, how did we do it, was that the best course back then, could we somehow correct some of the decisions, lives... what can we try to avoid in the future.* In this way, the memories would shape the future and how we can become whole again.

4

The Caine Workshop and African writing reflections: How I decided on "Notes from Mai Mujuru's breast".

I got an email from Lizzy Attree. She is the administrator of The Caine prize for African writing. She was inviting me to the workshop. She said I had been commended to her by Veronique Todjo. I didn't know this person. So at first I said to myself, "Surely, this is one of those hacking letters. They must want my laptop, or maybe my identity papers?"

I had been hacked before, two years before. Someone had assumed my name, and had even opened a bank account, then asked my family and friends to pay for my travel money from Madrid. I had lost my ticket money back to Zimbabwe, so I was stranded, from some workshop, at Madrid international airport. A cousin, David Mwanaka, almost coughed out the 2000 pounds they were saying I needed. David decided, at that last moment before payment to phone me on my South African numbers to find whether I really was stranded. I was safely ensconced in South Africa. So I thought this was another one.

In the letter, Lizzy, or this swindler, said we should bring our laptops. I had just procured one for myself and you must know how I felt if I were to lose it! Not that it is a huge thing. I thought this hacker was going to steal it from me at Harare international airport if I was going by the plane, or maybe at Beitbridge Border Post. I replied her though, just for the love of it, the love that I was that recognised to be selected and invited (some part of me really believed it. I am a doubter-believer), or just for the hacking and stealing job play-off. You should be special to be thus identified, even for that!

Then I started communicating with Jenny, for the ticket bookings and the Visa. Jenny and Lizzy are not the same names, so I distrusted it all the more. I lied to her that I needed a Visa, even though I knew there was no Visa between Zimbabwe and South Africa, to delay things a bit, to figure things out. I also had an infraction on my passport; I hadn't stamped my passport out, 4 years before, even though I had returned back to Zimbabwe. I had overstayed in South Africa during those years we would get days, or at most, a month's right to stay in South Africa at the border, so you had to travel every month from where you will be in South Africa to Beitbridge Border Post to have your passport stamped out, and there is a time I couldn't afford travelling every month from Johannesburg to the border so I had stopped having my passport stamped out, thus when I finally abandoned staying in South Africa for good, I sneaked illegally out of the country without proffering my passport that had an infraction, for stamping, and thus, I never was stamped out of South Africa. Thus now, I thought I might need some document when begging to the corrupt passport people to validate why I had to be in South Africa, when actually, according to my passport, I was still in South Africa. I have never really left the place! I have never enjoyed getting fleeced. But with the passport people its fine. I have done that before, at Beitbridge Border Post. So, I said to myself.

"Jenny now! Surely this thief really is going to such lengths!"

Then the ticket came through and I still didn't believe it. After all, there were internet tickets that I got, so I didn't know whether to believe them, or to just think he was doing a great job of fooling me. I don't want to call him a HE, as if SHE doesn't apply. But I had started already calling him HE. Men are generally good at this, are they not? Then Lizzy started talking to me again. I discovered I wasn't the only one who was going to be thieved on, no. I no longer believed the hacking theory. After all how could he try to fleece writers from all over the continent, at the same time? I started telling myself, THIS IS IT. I started telling people, well friends and the family about this. I got congratulations all around. Some even requested for a few dollars. I told them it was a writing workshop, not a writing award. I started thinking, obsessing about it all. I had never attended a writing workshop before. I didn't know what we will be doing other than, of course producing the stories. I have never been in the middle of people like me, writers? What? Crazies, strange people, no! It's easier to tell yourself you are not strange. Can you tell eleven others that they are not strange? I also started obsessing about which story I was going to write under those strict conditions.

There were some notes I had made three years before that I kept returning to, obsessively. I had been doing that for the past three years without going all the way in creating a story out of them. I don't usually make notes when I want to write a story. I just have an idea of what I am going to write about, and then I plough in. if I make notes usually it's always difficult for me to write the story…. it's as if I get dry in my head. The way about these notes was to produce a straight-forward kind of story, writing… and I didn't want to do that. I didn't want to please no editor, no instructor, no critic, no. They always want their work served in a nice platter, straightforwardish. I have had so many fights with these, and got on the wrong end of it all. Come on, there are just as strange as writers. Believe me you: They always want to select material they want (not need) to show and feel that they should cut quite a lot of the crap in the story. I rest my case!

I still didn't know other ways to go about those notes, and that's why I have been all over the landscape in this story (essay). It doesn't feel like a story, anymore. Writing a story! I find it, I think it's like a big blue sky, no clouds, nothing prescribed, and you can come from whichever side, without getting blocked because they are no clouds to block you. You can see your way through the skies of your imaginations, writing... Dambudzo Marechera thought of it as one foot, one big foot with many toes, little tiny toes. *Chimamanda Adichie's* warned against *The Danger of the Single Story, Youtube.com, 7 October 2009*, "when we reject the single story, when we realise that there is never a single story about any place, we regain a kind of paradise". We have to come from anywhere, go anywhere we want with our stories. Ok, enough of this! I am sure this is what my colleagues at the workshop and the facilitators would be saying whilst I will be reading this story, I thought, as I wrote this story and completed it in two hours, two days after we had started the workshop. I also want to ask, is it a story, as such? They want to hear the story. So, here is the story.

He was nineteen, Chris was, in those notes that I have obsessed about. It was three years ago when he was 19. He had no money; nobody had money in Zimbabwe, then. It was at the height of the problems in Zimbabwe, I mean the political problems. Those were the only problems to talk of in Zimbabwe, that's all we ever knew of. People were scuttling all over Zimbabwe, trying to eke out an existence, "not surviving, no. I can't even think of living, no. you just had to exist, and people can exist in all sorts of levels...." *Notes from Mai Mujuru's Breast*, in *Finding a Way Home, 2015*. In the story, *Dear Life, Dear*

Death in *Finding a Way Home*, I wrote, "Breathing is not even the base for existence…" I stop it!

When he told me the story, Chris had just jumped the South African border; a couple of months earlier to join us, unannounced, in South Africa. I will come to that. I have to disregard this toe at the present moment. Before he came to South Africa, he also went where all the other people were going those days in Zimbabwe, to eke out an existence. The people, or the whole of the country, were going to Marange. Way back, growing up in the rural areas of Nyatate, in Nyanga, in the Eastern Highlands of Zimbabwe, this name Marange had meant something totally different, or maybe the same thing with what people were going there for those days. In my little village of Mapfurira, and in my clan (I was told that this term has colonial meaning so I revised it in the story, *Notes from Mai Mujuru's breast* when it was being edited for inclusion in the novel, *Finding a Way Home*, to *family*), the Mwanakas, the bulk of which, were of the sect of Johanne Marange apostolic church. They tell you there are a Christian church, but don't take it at face value. The one who formed it called himself Johanne Wokutanga, meaning the first Johanne. Maybe there is to be a second Johanne? He was from Marange. By the way Marange is still in the Eastern Highlands, and it was where diamonds were being discovered. People were going there to mine diamonds illegally, to just receive this spiritual manna from heaven that had just sprouted out of the nowheres of the soils skies.

This apostolic sect had, and it still has them, strange beliefs. They believe in polygamy. My younger cousins have now at least 4 wives each and I have none. It's crazy, maybe both ways. Ok. They also believe for illnesses, problems, troubles, everything, they just have to pray and everything will be solved.

What solution? Even those that are not solved, in their minds they are solved, like if someone dies it was just-meant-to-be-solution. No medicines, no therapy, nothing about visiting N'angas (a traditional healer), nothing about anything, really.

Even the girls are not allowed to go to school past grade seven. They should have been married by then, and to an old church elder, especially prophets. Prophets, prophets, prophets..., its big business in Zimbabwe, to be a prophet now, and the sycophantic newspapers in Zimbabwe follows the predictions of these prophets and write endlessly about their shenanigans, and thus embolden these upstarts, thus they proclaim new and newer predictions. I think we should create a tournament for these guys, seeing who has gumption enough to lie. Lately another of these prophets, Prophet Emmanuel Makandiwa, ummmm, he once threatened to walk on top of Kariba Dam's waters, has now predicted Zimbabwe will soon be super rich with discovery of vast oil reserves, hahaha. I leave this toe.

To the Marange story: There was this prophet and he wanted this beautiful girl so he decided to win her using his position. In the church, he prophesies to the girl, telling her that she should go to the Baobab tree, out into the fields and pray under the tree, and that God will give her a vocation. Whatever God tells her she should do likewise. The girl did as she had been told to do, and was praying fervently. She hadn't even checked the tree to see what was inside it, up above her. The prophet was surely in this tree waiting for the girl to come. So when the girl was praying so hard, asking for revelation, the prophet bellowed in a huge voice from up the tree, telling the girl her prayers were being heard, and that she had to listen well to God's words. He told her she was set aside for a great promise. The promise was she was going to conceive a prophet for the church; and the son will be the son of the current prophet, meaning him, so the girl had to marry the prophet. This prophet had succeeded using his prophetic position and got the girl of his heart.

Young men in this church have always been second choice to girls. After all it's bloody survival of the fittest, in the church. Young people were not allowed to be prophets, up until now. Now, even a crying baby can claim to be a prophet, if it knows how to cry that well in Zimbabwe. And it would have thousands of followers within a huff, that's Zimbabwe and the confused Zimbos for you! Prophets in this church were the ones who would tell everyone what to do, who to get married to, and old man were always at an advantage. Ok, I will go back on Marange again.

This church would have its annual Pasika (Passover) at Marange. They would go there, huge families, to spend a month out there meditating, or not really doing that. It was also an opportunity for the old prophetic men to parade their new acquisitions, new wives, and to drink lots of tea and battered bread. That's all they ever really do out there. It usually happens in the colds of July, but it's not really cold in Marange. It's a bloody hot pit down there. It's in region 5, though the surrounding areas are in region 1, because it's a huge hot valley. You don't grow crops there. Crops, I mean any other crops, than Rapoko and Mhunga, which sometimes don't exist (I mean grow) beyond germination. So, to these Johannes Marange members going to Marange represented a spiritual journey like Moses would go into the wilderness to pray. Moses, Mosses, Moses, I will not talk about him.

Marange is a wilderness of some sort. Three years ago Johanne Marange sect members went to Marange for their annual Pasika and it was at the height of the cholera epidemic that swept through the country. It swiped these members. My own family lost over 21 people who don't even make the purported 5000 deaths recorded throughout the country. They don't believe people should be recorded. They never even acquired the birth certificates to start with so they didn't need death certificates. They were stubborn in their prayers. Even the Old Bones was stubborn in his belief that there was no cholera in Zimbabwe. I think all I ever thought of that place was about praying until people started going there for different reasons.

Chris was going there for this different reason as well. Chris, for Christopher Kanjunju was going there to find the ngodas, or the coveted "glass" diamonds. He is a distant relative. It's even too distant; it has run way from me to start describing it for you here. How related we were! I can't even explain it. But we had stayed together at the same place and street, such that it would have appeared as if the relationship was a very close one. It was very close, even closer than those I was closely related to, after all, it's the close friendship that's more important than a biological relationship that is far removed.

Then, the whole country was descending on Marange for the stones, ngodas and the coveted glass diamonds. Glass is the very best diamond, and it would fetch a lot.

Chris left by the train at about 9 at night for Mutare, with no spare shirt, no spare whatever, no food, no spare money, nothing. The trains were safer because they were not stopped on the road blocks by the police. They would leave you in Mutare so you would approach Marange from another side, less guarded, than using the direct road from Harare. In Mutare, he met someone going to Chiadzwa, in Marange and accompanied this someone such that he couldn't get lost on the way. They were ferried by a big truck going to Chipinge which they disembarked from at Chikohwa (in fact its Chakohwa, I was given this wrong spelling by Chris, which I mistakenly used in the Caine story, later corrected in *Finding a Way Home*), and walked by foot, a distance of over 50 km, crossed Odzi River and arrived at about 6 in the evening. Oh, stop hassling about these corrections I am making, the Caine story was a fictitious tale, and I was within my rights to create any factitious names I wanted, even mistakenly so, but in this essay I have to record everything correctly!

Chris also said the whole place, the whole Chiadzwa diamond fields had been parcelled into four parts. The first part was known as Mufakose (Mufakose literally means "die in everything". I should think it had been named after Mufakose high density township in the western dusty and dirty bowls of Harare. Some critic is gnashing his/her teeth saying that we should write about Africa in a less pessimistic and disparaging way...oh some critic even referred me to read Wainana Bainyanga's writings on this portraying of Africa in a less harsher way. I wonder what about the truth, who is going to do that for Africa. Ummm, the Western World! And who would believe them, when everyone in Africa is trying to liar about Africa. Can you tell someone he has shitted on himself and would that person accept it as dirty when that person has come to take it as clean. No Bainyanga, I shall write the truth as it is, Africa or no Africa.

The dirty Mufakose was the place where you could get ngodas, a poor cheap form of diamonds, an "industrial" diamond. Even Mufakose Township hugs the industrial area in Harare. The second part was known as Mbare (also named after the notorious high density slum of Harare. It had the same issues like Mufakose). The third part was known as

Mbada (named after the leopard. Mbada, the leopard, is of the cat family, with so beautiful spots. Maybe it was for the beauty of the spots, so also the beauty of the glass diamond found in this spot that it was thus named). The fourth part was known as Zamu raMai Mujuru (literary meaning, "Mai Mujuru's breast". A breast to a little kid or even to an old man represents life, living, loving. I am not going into details on what a breast represent to men. I don't want to be labelled a sexist pig).

Mai Mujuru is the Vice president of Zimbabwe. The wife of the late Army General Solomon Mujuru (burned in an inferno at his farm house in political conspiracy and ZANU-PF factions' power manoeuvrings). Solomon Mujuru was seen as the head of the Mujuru's faction which is fighting with the Mnangagwa's faction (the defence minister) for the presidency, if and when if, the Old Bones folds down into mother earth. The Mujuru's were mining this area known as Mai Mujuru's breast. There are still there but have hidden behind other names, in fact, nowadays there is only one name being heard there, Mbada diamond mining company. Maybe they have joined the Mai Mujuru's breasts and the leopard, and it's an awesome combination. There are no sexual innuendoes here.

Chris was staying in Mufakose; everyone was staying in Mufakose those days. The whole country was staying in Mufakose, mining whatever little ngodas they could scrounge around and eke out an existence. And you expect someone staying in Mufakose to write flattering things about a country that has abandoned him or her to Mufakose! But some poor people developed ambitions. Some didn't abide the idea of staying in Mufakose for the rest of their lives so they started foraging into, fondling, caressing, licking, the pig wire fence that surrounded Mai Mujuru's breast and the Mbada area. Chris said these two places were fenced off, with the police, the army, the fearsome CIO, and the green bombers (the marauding ZANU-PF youths.) were doing a 24hr guarding of the place. Inside the fence the place was made up of heaped-up lumps, mounds, of the coveted glass diamond and soil. The huge mounds were the ones referred to as Mai Mujuru's breast. If you lick a bit of that breast, you go home smiling to the bank and vault yourself off the Mufakose Township into the lush, leafy northern suburbs of Harare. How do you get to lick Mai Mujuru's huge mounds? You bribe the police on duty and the sums were huge. One policeman was found with a hefty US$44 000 after an 8 hrs guarding duty, so it meant for the lot of the Mufakose residence they couldn't afford this or so they stayed down there in Mufakose, besides the industries and "industrial" diamonds.

For those with the money, they would bribe the police with this money and would be given under an hour to get through, even through the gates, or cut the wire, and grab whatever piece of Mai Mujuru's breast and clear out before capture. Those bribed policemen would sound off warning by blasting their riffles into the air, and the bribers would know they have to run out of Mai Mujuru's abundant lick. The bribed police would only sound warning if their superiors were coming to inspect them before the one hour interval expired, or after the hour of foraging through Mai Mujuru's breast was over. One hour should be a lot of time to make love to Mai Mujuru! Those who got rich from Marange got rich doing this. Those who remained poor stayed, and are still staying in Mufakose and Mbare.

Chris didn't have the money to bribe these police people so he had to dance around them, even in his Mufakose area. There were run-ins with the police. The police didn't want anyone near Mai Mujuru's breast and this Mufakose and Mbare area was too closer rather than the actual Mbare and Mufakose townships which were a bit far away from Mai Mujuru's breast, or even the Old Bones' home. They wanted everyone to go back to the actual Mufakose and Mbare, way-back in Harare, over 300 km away. So the battles in this Mufakose were so like a country at war.

Chris and his Mufakose people stayed away from the area during the day, and slept off, at the nearby shops. At night they would invade this Mufakose area, and meet with the police, run off to the nearby mountains, return back later, dig a little bit, meet with the police, run off, return a little bit later, continue digging their hole, the first day without success. You would dig a bit of some soil, pack it in your plastics and run off, then the morrow morning you would wash it with water and find, nothing! Sometimes they dared invading the place in the afternoons and the battles would assume war status with the police. A lot of people were killed, in fact for the 6 days he was there they were at least 5 deaths every day. People were also being beaten up by the police; some were eaten alive by the police dogs. Then they devised a new method to deal with the dogs. When they were being chased they would urge the dogs to chase them far away from the police, and then stone the dog dead or give it poisoned meat. And the battles continued along those lines.

The second day Chris tried again and got nothing. He didn't tire. The third day he tried again, got his pocketful of soil, washed it in the morning of the fourth day, and found his first ngoda, which he sold for Z$600 billion dollars, bought food, i.e. only bread and milk for that amount. That fourth day he went to the fields energised a bit after having his first real meal in over three days but got nothing. He tried again on the fifth day and got nothing. He didn't stop. On the sixth day he tried again and got nothing. The bread and milk was out so he couldn't think of spending some more days eating wild fruits, again. He sold his stuff that is the shoes, a shirt, a cell phone and returned back home in Mufakose Harare, with just the trousers and panties. Chris didn't give up. He stole his mother's cell phone, a couple of electronic things at home, traded these and board a truck off to South Africa, bribed some border gangsters at around Limpopo river to help him cross into South Africa illegally. He was stripped off everything except his clothes and abandoned just after crossing Limpopo by those border gangsters and had to find his way through by foot to Musina refugee camp. He processed a refugee permit worth only six months and phoned my brother that he needed some bus fare money to Johannesburg and a place to stay. My brother sent him the money and he came to stay with us. That was almost three years ago.

I made those notes almost three years ago and have failed to create a story about them. I still didn't know whether this was a story? But when it had settled down to me that I was going to the workshop I thought a lot about writing about Chris. I also thought, that it had happened too long ago. The cholera that had devastated the Johanne Marange sect members had gone too. Mai Mujuru's breast had shrivelled into Mbada diamond mining company. I haven't been to our rural home for years, almost 6 years now, so Marange doesn't connect to my childhood anymore. I haven't been there to meet those of my family left off after the cholera scourge who would definitely remind me of the spiritual connotations of Marange. I thought, maybe, I could write about the killing of Mujuru. At least I will still be closer to Mai Mujuru's breast. But, they had since separated by the time he was killed, though they kept up appearances as husband and wife. I have diverged again!

The Caine Workshop was enjoyful, the environment and the place we were stationed was heavenly as I described it in the upcoming essay, *My Volmoed Journey*. So I will try to spare you that in this essay. I want to focus more on the actual writing of the piece, the reading, the critiquing of our work. The critiquing was very friendly and comforting for a beginning writer. We would critique each other softly, as if we were afraid of making enemies of each other, sometimes I found it a bit patronising. We would meet after dinner (dinner was at 6 every night) and 3 writers would read their stories and we would critique those writers, offering advice, help etc. Nick Elam (outgoing Caine administrator) and breeze Lizzy Attree (incoming administrator) would lead this reviewing process, with help from our instructors, Jamal and Henrietta. But it was open affair, writers were encouraged to express their opinions, though as I noted it was too respectful. The instructors would help us during the day hours as we worked on our pieces, trying to shape our work.

It is very beneficial to work with someone at that close range who would help you in crafting the story, you tend to avoid a lot of the pitfalls that you would encounter when working alone, through this open generation of ideas on how to move the story ahead, and editing it (which I want to admit I learned a lot more about from our instructors. I tend to make a lot of grammatical errors and it would take me a lot of editing to weed them out when I am working alone). Here it was half a job done for they helped me a lot on that.

But working with someone closely has its problems. It depends with the kind of instructor, just like editing itself. Some editors have a heavy-on approach so are some instructors, some keep a bit of distance to allow the writer to write. I protested when I felt I didn't want to follow their suggestions, but for a writer who is a bit timid, there is a danger in the instructor taking over and becoming more the writer, and thus the stories produced wouldn't help the writer much (in the future), in figuring how to write better. And resultantly you might end up creating the same stories (sameness in writing) in the anthology because the writers have become lost (have lost control to the instructors) to their stories. I think this is what *Shimmer Chinodya*, in *Panorama Magazine, 2014, Online*, feels there is no growth with the writers coming out of the Caine award and workshop. Even in our group there are few now left producing work regularly. The problem might be with the selection process or just that pursuing writing is an arduous task. There are a few of the winners or even the shortlisted writers who have sustained output as writers, over the years, and developed into professional writers. The lot die with that first recognition that the award accords those selected.

It's not just the Caine. It's a lot other awards on offer in Africa. The problem could really be on selection criteria, where writers really deserving of the awards are overlooked for the cooked winners who usually follow rules and write specifically to win awards, not to develop into a balanced and professional writer. That's why we are replete with one book wonders in Africa. The problem stems from the administrators (board, instructors, selectors, and judges) trying to define what a writer should address and how they have to address it (the *Positivication* of Africa school, I have discussed before), and thus already those who portray Africa poorly (in the eyes of these judges) whether it is the truth or not, are already out of the running, despite their talents, thus already it's a cooked-up award and a cooked-up writer will most likely win it. Yet, it's one thing to win or be shortlisted for an award and another to write consistently and write things that stay the test of time and develop into a professional.

There is too much reliance on judging writers from awards won, yet it is significant scholarship that we should be encouraging from our writers. I don't want to be hearing every time I hear of a writer; it's always about his or her one novel that I hear of. That's why I have huge respect for awards that look at a body of work from a writer and award a writer for these, like the Nobel, DAAD Fellowships etc. Africa is still at the formative stage of writing where we have to open out and unearth as many of our millions of passionate writers out there by giving them an opportunity to grow, rather than the award's arbitrary way of selecting one or two winners and the rest are junked off. I think the focus should be more on creating opportunities for writers to have their work published and with continual publishing a writer grows from learning from fellow writers published in these, it could be literary journals, magazines, webpages, anthologies etc. These really can make a change in a writer's journey. I grew as a writer from participating in these journals, especially in the USA, which is replete with these platforms, and that's no wonder American writers develop better than all us. It is because America has a lot of these platforms to unearth and groom a writer.

The last area I want to focus on is this pervading sense I have had for years that these awards seem to have created monarchies of some sort in writing. It's easy for a writer who has connections, literary connections to be awarded an award, than one who is not really connected. It's an amalgam connection between the publishers, the award givers, the establishment, the media, the writers, and we tend to see writers coming from these connected worlds winning. As can be noted with this year where a writer who has won the Caine has been shortlisted again for the Caine, really! You mean he so talented to beat another hundreds of entries coming from all over the continent. And at one time, in 2013, there were 4 writers from one country in the selections (Nigerians) and I was left to wonder is Nigeria 4 times more talented than the whole of Africa combined together or there is really something wrong with the whole system.

5

My Volmoed Journey

pic courtesy by Waigwa Ndiangui

When it had sunk in that I would definitely be going to the Cape, for the Caine African writers' workshop, I made the necessary preparations. I woke up very early, at around four o'clock in the morning of 5th March 2012. I had a flight to catch scheduled for seven o'clock from Harare. And my brother-in-law, Nicholas Tachiveyi took me to the airport in his personal car, before he proceeded to his workplace. It was my first time to go to the airport, let alone board a flight. Yet despite my anxieties, I discovered that the procedures at Harare International Airport were not complex.

In no time, we were taxing on the runaway. I hadn't buckled up and when the plane began its ascent I felt like I was floating on a giant Ferris wheel. I experienced a powerful thrust as my body fell back onto the seat. Our Boeing was flying the colours of the national carrier South African Airways. By the time we hit cruising speed was when I remembered to adjust my seat, then buckled up. I was thrilled. Unfortunately, from the middle seat I couldn't see much of the outside. I ate the food they provided and was even brave enough to have a coke, which I regretted later. My stomach reacted in violent cramps. Ordinarily I avoid drinks made with anything other than fresh ingredients. For certain preservatives tend to hurt my stomach.

As we approached O.R Tambo International Airport for landing, I marvelled at the airplane descending and curving. But for some it was scary. It dawned on me that I could enjoy flights more than road travel. Previously, car journeys sometimes made me retch badly. Without preamble we hit the runaway. It was a firm nudge as the plane made contact with the tarmac.

I had checked in my bag at Harare International Airport, so when we arrived in Johannesburg, I was embarrassed to note that people were taking their bags from the overhead baggage bins. I wondered whether mine would be there too, and I even ensured that I was last to exit the plane. I searched for my bag in all the compartments. I was so convinced that my bag had been stolen –until I checked with the flight attendant. She asked me whether I had brought it inside the plane with me. I said no. She then informed me that I should check for it on the arrivals carousel. I felt utterly embarrassed.

From Johannesburg to Cape Town

From O.R Tambo International Airport to Cape Town International Airport, I was comfortable. I had problems with undoing my belt though, luckily I was helped by a fellow passenger. That time, it wasn't that embarrassing. I don't usually get embarrassed, as I tend to rationalise such feelings. Things are simply normal even though I'm in fact a little ignorant about them, or find them too complex or strange.

The administrator of the Caine prize, Lizzy Attree, had said that we were to meet at the international arrivals hall. And that's where I was waiting for the others. But it seemed nobody had showed up yet. After an hour, I went to the phone booths and tried phoning her. But I couldn't reach her, and it made me quite desperate. Fortunately this episode was over two hours later when I walked up to a stranger selling treats at the international arrival hall. I asked him whether I could use his cell phone to call someone, and gladly discovered that he was Zimbabwean too. So we conversed in our language, Shona. It's in this spirit that he helped me connect with Lizzy. She directed me back to the domestic arrivals hall, where I had already checked several times for the group. I didn't know anyone in the group personally, moreover I had only linked up with two of the writers on Facebook –a few weeks earlier. I met Mehul Gohil and Lauri Kubuitsile before the three of us finally met up with the rest of our contingent.

The journey to Volmoed, Hermanus

Percy Tours took care of our travels. At around four in the afternoon, we were on our way to Hermanus, Volmoed, where we'd be spending the entire ten day workshop. The one and a half hour drive took us through some of the most beautiful scenery in South Africa. The landscape is scored with gorges, rivers and mountains. You sometimes see granite or limestone outcrops resembling bones jutting out from the mountains. Rivers at times shone like a silver scimitar cutting down through the mountains as they went down to the sea. Higher up on the mountains tended to be sparsely forested compared to the lush estuaries.

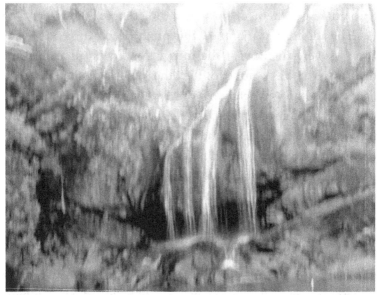

pic courtesy by Waigwa Ndiangui

When you drove ahead determinedly, it felt as though the sea threatened to gobble up all the land. Against it, smooth roads seamlessly wove through the landscape. In the light of falling sun, the surface of the sea was like a cracked or shredded but still intact pane of glass. In the evening light, everything was lent a halo of amber. It was an awesome sight to behold. And I was enjoying it immensely, despite my violently irritated stomach.

The car I was in was shared with a South African lady called Grace Khunou, a Kenyan lady called Brenda Mukami Kunga and Lizzy Attree. The rest were in the second car. Lizzy asked me about Dambudzo Marechera, the iconoclastic Zimbabwean writer. In the newspaper she had been reading there was an article written about Dambudzo. She mentioned something about how Dambudzo had infected Flora Viet Wild (his biographer) with HIV, and how it had taken her that long to spill the secret out. Which I later read about online in the essay *Me and Dambudzo: a personal essay* by *Flora Veit-Wild*. I could barely reply to Lizzy.

Lizzy couldn't have known how I was suffering inside.

I am sure she could have understood me to be just a shy person; in fact that's what she told me later on. Maybe, I am generally shy, but then it was made worse by the stomach cramps. Later I told Lizzie that I had never been to any ocean, let alone the sea. She was surprised. But that didn't bother me. I couldn't wait for the journey to end so that I could find relief.

Eventually we reached Hermanus. It's an awesome town with pretty buildings. Most were painted off-white, light grey or green, with a smattering of shades of brown in between. It was reminiscent to a Mediterranean Riviera setting – to me at least, or an Eastern European seaside town.

We stayed in Volmoed in the scenic Hemel en Aarde Valley, which is a 15 minute drive out of Hermanus. The Hermanus district is predominantly occupied by the coloured population. Culinary tastes are conventionally South African, which means there is an eclectic choice resultant from the diverse communities that make up this area. These ordinarily range from African foods, sauces and dressings to European continental tastes.

Hemel en Aarde literally means valley of heaven and earth, and I knew I was in a very special place. Once you are inside the valley, the vista appears to reach out to the heavens.

"This particular area in which Volmoed is located was earlier known as Attaquaskloof", says John and Isobel De Gruchy, 2006, in their book, The Volmoed Journey. "The name Attaqua means the place of Atta, which suggests that a Khoi people lead by someone known by the name Atta did, in fact, live here long enough for the area to be associated with him." In 1817, Lord Charles Somerset declared it a leper colony, turning the valley into a place of healing. Subsequently, the colony was moved in 1845 to Robben Island, the place Mandela would later be incarcerated for twenty seven years. Attaqua was subdivided into plots and sold off. One of the farms was named Volmoed, meaning "full of courage and hope". In 1986, the present Volmoed community purchased the farm. Bernard Tukstra currently runs it.

An unfortunate realisation struck me about the place; not much of the Khoi people's artefacts could easily be found around. Perhaps they had been obliterated by the white settlers as they systematically made advances against the Khoi. Perhaps the Khoi took their living secrets with them as they succumbed to new diseases, like small pox, for which they had no immunity. Franscesca Mitchel, Online, stated that "in 1713, an estimated 90 percent of the KhoiSan population is thought to have been wiped out by smallpox."

Most of the buildings at Volmoed have whitewashed walls and green roofs which seem to merge into the greenery. People were saying it had been the driest summer for years on the Overberg. Because that whole area is part of the Cape over-berg, it means temperatures are significantly influenced by ocean currents. At any moment, it could get pretty chilly even in summer. Generally it was warm when we stayed there, but all the green belied a worryingly dry summer for the locals.

In summer it's hot and windy while winter is cold and rainy. Sometimes there is snow, especially higher up in the mountains, one of which is the Babilonstoring range. At times the melt water triggered floods down in the valley.

Volmoed
Our cottages were named Keurboom, Vyeboom and Boekenhout. We shared a cottage among three —me and the Kenyans Mehul Gohil and Waigwa Ndiang'ui were in Keurboom. We each had a private bedroom, and shared the dinning/lounge, kitchen and toilet area. Outside our veranda was a leafy Keurboom tree.

These cottages are built cutting into the edge of the mountain. They merge into the mountain unobtrusively, testifying to the skill invested in the project. For they respect the scenery, and make themselves part of it. It was not difficult to feel artistic at Volmoed, for the scenery felt like the delightful work of art. But actually it's the spiritual centre of the Anglican Church of South Africa. People come there from all over South Africa and abroad on spiritual excursions. The staff at Volmoed were fabulous and very helpful, especially the owner and founder Bernard Turkstra, and the head chef Marie Philip. My stomach tends to be rather choosy, and it complained a bit, but after a few meals it was won over. I even sampled a new dish at every meal.

The Caine Story

I knew writing the story wasn't going to be impossible in that setting. Hence I didn't push myself as hard as I usually do. I lounged, ate well, slept well, and strolled the verdant grounds. Some writers – Waigwa in particular, joked that I came with a story already written. He argued that I was always fooling around while others were concentrating. That's because I completed my first draft in a day. And it was only the second day after we arrived. I wrote in a single sitting of two hours, all between four and six in the morning. I knew the instructors wouldn't like that but I went ahead and wrote it all the same. It was experimental and read almost like non-fiction.

My story was based on the discovery of diamonds at Marange and its exploitation between 2005 and 2006. It fuelled illegal mining, corruption and the not unanticipated killings of the artisanal miners by government forces. The larger story was to highlight how Zimbabwe was pillaged by the political establishment, through mismanagement and corruption. Marange had held the possibility of Zimbabwe's rise from its current economic crisis. But now, that dream had been confounded for the majority Zimbabweans.

Well, one instructor didn't like the story. OK, maybe they liked the humour, but the experimentation meant that other themes were trampling on the real story. Both my instructors, Henrietta Rose-Innes and Jamal Mahjoub advised me to write the story in a clear and linear way. Because I knew I could not enjoy doing that, I lost my initial excitement.

The scenery, flora and fauna

I was captivated by the breath-taking scenery. One day I followed the Onrus river back, up to the mountains. It originated in the Babilonstoring range, then filled the De Bos dam, before cascading over a waterfall. Along its valley, it paused into a small pool near a place called The Grotto. Ten kilometres later, it reached the Indian Ocean. Onrus means restless.

The Onrus is a gentle river, but sometimes after occasional snowfalls on the Babilonstoring Mountains, or after a particularly heavy rainy season, it can be restless; flooding the lower sections of Volmoed, washing away bridges, trees, and even drowning people. But the name came about because people down-stream feared that it might bring diseases from the leper colony. This made them anxious and restless, thus the name.

Bird life is abundant, and I saw some thrush, red-cocked woodpecker, yellow-billed ducks, doves, white backed ravens, witoogies, sunbirds, and the cape sugarbird. Other wild life found in this area include baboons, leopard – outside the park areas in the temperate Cape areas; especially in its mountainous areas, beetle, puff udder, cape cobra, boomslang, and reebok. We did create a lot of stories involving the baboons, and some of the more imaginative among us called them zombie baboons. Jamal and Lauri took the initiative to make up fantastical tales. Every night till late, we made up stories about how they might come and attack us.

The flora of this place is distinct. In this part of the Western Cape, flowers blossom throughout the year. The De Gruchys 2006, say,

> There are six floral kingdoms in the world and the Cape Floral Kingdom is the smallest of the six in extent. Eighty percent of it is made up of fynbos. The Cape Floral Kingdom covers an area comparable to the land mass of Malawi or Portugal and hosts 8600 plant species, 5800 of which are only found in this area. To put it into perspective, the British Isles, three and half times larger, have only 1500 plants species.

The most prominent plants I was looking out for were the fynbos, aristaes, proteas, white and mauve ericas, keurboom and smaller keurtjies, snowdrops, brilliant yellow daisy bushes, white plums, the imposing magnolias, camellia, azalea, stately oak trees in their new leaves, roellas, aulax putting out their feathery yellow stamens, orange ursinia, and the tiny geissorhia.

On this journey up the river, I was with Beatrice Lamwaka, a Ugandan writer. We walked up midway the journey with Waigwa. He preferred to return to Volmoed to work on his story. Beatrice and I talked mostly about writing, her work as reviewer of books in Uganda, the literary scene in her country, and their promising publishing initiative with Femrite.

I really wanted to get into the waterfall or at the very least get close enough to touch it. When I got near it, I felt like I was a part of it. Below was a deep green pool. I was not sure how deep, but anything that appeared too deep has always scared me. So I could not begin to imagine what might lie inside. I imagined water animals that I'm not fond of: snakes, mermaids, and crocodiles. But, I was mostly scared of the Njuzu (mermaid) that day, so we enjoyed it from the outside. It's not a joke, I am afraid of these aquatic half human creatures. In my culture and country, these creatures are associated with supernatural forces, for instance it is believed the most potent traditional healers is of the Njuzu calling. It is said that they were often people who had been abducted by a Njuzu and secreted deep inside caves, in the river's pools, where they would be taught the trade. So growing up, we were always afraid of river pools that were said to have Njuzu in them. Afraid we might be abducted by these supernatural creatures. It is also believed that should people mourn for you after your abduction, these creatures would kill you. Thus you can understand my fear of these creatures at that instance.

The sea, the sea

On the only day that we left our abode, we had an afternoon excursion to explore the area in the vicinity of the Clemsburg River. We boarded The African Queen, a large, two storied river boat. I remained on the lower deck. Because I had never been to the sea, I requested Lizzy to take us there. She recommended Grotto beach. Since I had never been to the sea or ocean, I took it as a thoughtful present.

The water was chilly but I got inside and waded for nearly an hour. It struck me that beaches are not actually blue, as depicted in pictures. This one had white sands and where the waves crashed, the water was off grey, but clean. Then we frolicked on the beach until it was time to return to Volmoed. As we passed through Hermanus again, we caught sight of intriguing public art and a beautiful brown tiled chapel.

pic courtesy by Waigwa Ndiangui

To see the dam

March 14 was our last full day at Volmoed, by which date we had finished writing our stories. To mark this milestone, Brenda, Beatrice, Waigwa and I climbed nearby mount Kleinbergie. It lies just a short distance across the Onrus river. We wanted to see the mountain and the dam.

In the previous year's Caine Anthology, South African Ken Barris had written a story *To see the Mountain*. It was based on his attempt to climb mount Cameroon. We felt we were on a similar jaunt. But what was additionally driving me and Waigwa was the desire to see the dam. We had been told there was a dam on top of the mountains, the De Bos dam. As we ascended, we found The Pine Pond midway up the mountain. It was full of wild flowers and weeds. We argued for minutes whether this was the dam or not. Eventually we concluded that it was too small to be a dam. We agreed to keep climbing the mountain, rather than take another path away from this range. I realised belatedly that that path would have gotten us right up to the dam. Brenda was too tired to go on, so we decided to abort our trip. We hadn't found the dam. As we descended, at the pond we found Rehana Rossouw. Since she is South African, we asked her whether that was the dam. Just to be sure. She said it was and all our arguments ended. Waigwa and I still believed that there was a bigger dam out there. For both of us, there was this sense that we had failed on our quest to conquer the mountain, or even to find a proper dam.

Heaven on earth

Rehana told us there was a chapel, The Thanksgiving Chapel, to the other side of our writing retreat. Since I hadn't been to that other side, she offered to take us there. I had already seen the two prayer places; The Prayer Hut on top of the mountain, and The Prayer Grotto, on the edge of the river.

Both places were mystical to me. They inspired feelings that overwhelmed me. Both The Prayer Hut and the Prayer Grotto lay amidst the burial ground of the faithful who had lived in the area. In certain places lay urns bearing the ashes of the departed.

I tend to be pensive in burial grounds. Sometimes I've had a feeling that the person buried down below can see and pity me. There was an element of fear and being laid bare at the same time. So, I didn't stay for long at both places.

The same anxiety gripped me in the chapel. But the presence of other people comforted me. The chapel grounds had an array of flowers and a pond accentuated by a well cut lawn. I imagined it as a place I might marry at one day. But I knew it would be a long way till then. As the chapel was closed to visitors on that day, we had no opportunity to explore what mysteries lay inside. Later, I read that it is filled with art and artefacts, some of which had come all the way from Zimbabwe. One of the notable pieces was a curved crucifix donated by a Mr. Roger Hickley. In that sense, it might not really have been a long way away for me.

As we sat on the lawn a while later, several local cats approached us. I reached out and petted one with white fur, in spite of not being fond of cats.

Journey back to earth

The following day, the workshop ended. I left with the first group of writers who had morning flights out. I left for Cape Town international airport and waited for my afternoon flight to Johannesburg. The rain was pelting down as I stepped off the plane. I had decided to make a short stay in Johannesburg, with the intention of seeing my brother and his family, and our extended family in the neighbourhood.

On the return leg to Zimbabwe, I got the window seat. This time round it was truly awesome to be airborne. Fabulous cloud formations drifted past and at times they were below me. I imagined touching them, experiencing their cotton softness. These ranged from shades of grey to dusty brown, and sometimes we cut though storm clouds that shook the aircraft with turbulence. It was the sight of Chitungwiza city from high above that I enjoyed most, because it is essentially a well arranged village. Chitungwiza city is dormitory residential city 26 Kilometres south of Harare. Some of our most popular Zimbabwean artists hail from there. These artists include among others: Charles Mungoshi, John Chibadura, Alick Macheso, Leonard Dembo, and Thomas Mapfumo. This neighbourhood is fondly known as the Hollywood of Zimbabwe.

The Hunyani River appeared like it was an artist's impression of a blue string. Its source is around the Marondera area and flows between Harare and Chitungwiza, all the way down to Norton town. And then, we were taxing at Harare International Airport. My journey to Volmoed, the Western Cape had ended.

6

Nyanga, December 2015:
In Search of Ancient Ways

Every few years I make this journey back to where I came from like an eel. There is no regular pattern to these going-home travels. And I haven't been doing that during the Christmas holidays in a long while. I last was home during Christmas holidays, 9 years ago, so it was with great anticipation when I decided to go home for the Christmas break in 2015. It's no longer such a horrendous journey as the transport system has improved with possibilities of getting a taxi to Nyanga in almost every hour of the day from Harare, which is 300kms away, where I stay. The easiest way is to hike, several times, all the way, and that's what I did on the 24th December 2015.

I took a half-bus taxi to Rusape, which is 200kms from Harare, and then I took another taxi to Nyanga town, about 75km from Rusape, and finished off with another half-bus taxi from Nyanga Town to home, in Nyatate, Mapfurira village, which is about 35kms from Nyanga Town, so my journey went smoothly, and I arrived at our rural shops, Nyatate shopping centre, at around 12 in the afternoon. It was an uneventful journey, and things seemed the same way they were since the last 2 years I hadn't been there.

This summer it wasn't raining for some time, and crops were barely germinating in most fields, and the talk of a draught was the talk all around, and funny when we had reached Nyatate that's when it started raining. All along the journey, it never gave any sign it was going to rain, until we were in the Nyanga area that's when we started seeing those dangerous eastern rain clouds fermenting in the skies with so much menace

And usually in this eastern part of Zimbabwe the skies don't fume for a long time before they explode, maybe because it is a mountainous place and rain can easily come down from any of the mountain ranges, especially the majestic Nyanga mountain. In less than an hour we were hit by a rain wave that started in the Nyanga Mountain to the east, and it followed the range down from Bende gap, all down to Chinyamusaka gap, then it moved west into our villages and it swept across the western part of Nyanga area where my home is. The lucky thing is when it started raining we were in the taxi, but the worse thing was by the time I reached my bus stop, which is 100 metres away from shelter at home, it was still ploughing heavily. I couldn't stay in the taxi, so I alighted to meet the rains. My father was waiting for me at our bus stop with 2 umbrellas. He gave me one of which, but in that minute or two it took me to collect my luggage form the taxi tout I had already been sogged, so I didn't care to hide under the umbrella. I braced the rain for the few metres to shelter.

25 December 2015

I am home again, after 2 years away from the place. I am home for the Christmas holidays. Since December 2006 holidays I haven't been home during this time. One thing that strikes me instantly as I woke up on the 25th is I am off the screen world, in a long time, 2 years of it! The only screen thing I have is my cell phone which is out most of the times due to the battery; no electricity here so we are all depending on a small solar panel. It's very quiet here, birds exploding in the tress, hens clucking, cocks cocking, and the distant hum of voices in other rooms, houses, homes, and the ever-present voices of my mum and dad, and Delight, the second-cousin they stay with.

The place feels larger, there are trees all around our home, my family practice a balanced reservation (conservation) system on the use of trees in our plots and we have always made an effort to keep trees. I love trees, my father loves trees. The trees are a green of summer. It rained yesterday so every animal, every tree is happy. I am very calm, cool, very much in sweet solitude with the place. I hope it will fuel my creativity batteries. I haven't been writing much as there are a lot of other things, including the business part of writing that claims more of my attention when I am in the city. I don't have a lot of time when I am in the city to really have a go at writing. So what I am looking for is the appetite to start writing and breathing well. Yes I am breathing beautiful oxygen air, free of pollution.

In this morning I got a goat for the Christmas meals and food. It was just a process to acquire food for me, even though I can't say I enjoyed it. Fletching the skin was a bit laborious. In this morning I am also going to the Christmas Mass at my oldest parish (outstation), St Michaels Gwanyan'wanya. I haven't been to Mass at this church like in a long, long time, maybe about 2004; I don't even remember the last time. I know I won't be able to recognise a lot of people, but I want to see what I see.

26 December 2015

I had a great yesterday, listening to the old, old songs; choral, mystical, spiritual music I grew up singing. And the Mass still had old ways of doing it, the response and calls were old, I harked back to the past. Where I stay in Chitungwiza, in Harare province, we have moved into the new ways of response and call, and the songs are more modern, new, immediate, happy, sometimes lacking in soul, in fact there are too many new songs per year and this new music takes centre stage in Mass in the cities, but here in the rural settings it's the old ways that dominate and it is so soul fulfilling and beautiful. Old people too, and I meet a lot of them. They are guys I grew up with, mothers and fathers I knew back then, kids we left and they are now grownups. They were all amazed and excited to see me again. I have always been popular in my village and the surrounding villages. Some hadn't seen me in over 20 years, some 9. As I noted before I haven't been home this time of the year in 9 years, even when I would come home once in a while, and even in December 2006, I didn't go, couldn't go to church on that Christmas period, so all I could see were a few neighbourly people in those instances.

Then I return home, took some pics of the mountain range, Muchena Mountains, and the lower Nyanga range and Chinyamusaka gap, the villages nestled quietly below the mountains, goats bleating, scrounging for tree leaves, people walking from the church back to their homes, the thatched huts, the asbestos roofed houses, the cattle kraals, the constant hum of voices, bird calls, the distant laughter, the sun in the skies, a beautiful summer sky, blue. This is a beautiful place, and it's easier to take it for granted if you stay in this place. Yes, Nyanga is considered a tourist destination area, with a lot of hotels concentrated on the south part of Nyanga, around Nyanga Town. They are several tourist attraction sites in the beautiful idyllic mountainous Nyanga area, like the World's View, where you can see as far as Headlands and Mashonaland from that point, then there is Troutbeck fishing resort, closer to our homes the old Ziwa Ruins, the Pungwe, Nyangombe and Mutarazi falls, Nyanga National Park. Nyanga Mountain to the east of me is redolent in ever-changing colours depending with the sun, the cloud cover, the atmospherics. It always is a sight of great beauty. I think you can spend the whole day photographing it as it changes colours.

One moment its dawn blue, the next it is misty blue, rainy blue, rusty red blue (from the setting sun), the rainbow arching across it, and then it is dusky blue, then blackish blue with the dusky becoming deep evening. Even at full night it's visible in many colours, and in the morning it is volcanic brilliant yellowish as the sun sprouts from, it seems, a deep hole within it.

Today, after breakfast, I walk to the nearby mountains (it's a group of hills really). In the middle of all Nyatate villages, to the east is Mapfurira village (my home village), and Chibvuri, to the south is Mukwaira and Dandadzi villages, to the west is Tenga, Sanyabako and Saunyama villages, to the north is Gwanyan'wanya, Chidazuru Kanyuru and Nyabeze villages, and on top of these hills you can see all the villages, arranged beautiful, and further these villages into other villages like Mapako, Tamunesa, Hogo, etc.... and beyond into the Rusape area too. You can see as far to Nyanga Town (35 km), as far as Chinyamusaka, as far Ruchera in Rusape, and the interminglingly and intertwining musics of the villages, rivers, hills mountains to create beauty. To the north are the mystical misty blue Muchena mountains, to the west is the balding old Ruchera dolomite mountains, to the east is of course Zimbabwe's biggest and highest mountain, Nyanga mountain (peaks at over 2 800 metres above sea level), and to the south is Turo, Ziwa and Nyahukwe Mountains. I have written about this place before in several pieces, especially the poem, *Sights, Thought and Feelings*, in the collection Playing to Love's Gallery (2016) which I will quote below

> During early spring one sits on top of-
> Musumburera hill, a large flat rock towering,
> In sight of beautiful villages of Nyatate.
> Languidly to the east, a sleeping lion stretches.
> Such a creature, undulating terrain with wonderful-
> Curvy dark valleys, downward flowing, beautifully.
> Trees dense, grass tall, inaccessible terrain-
> It's the ages old Nyanga Mountain.

Ruchera Mountain keeps balding old to the west and intermingling with other small hills, streams, and rivers to hold and form food to the eyes, so delicious and tasty. South are the Nyahukwe and Ziwa Mountains, which are always a shade lighter bluer, like disappearing mist and to the north are the blue and rainy..., Muchena Mountains, sources of the summer's abundant rains that nourish this glorious beautiful vistarama.

It is impossible not to feel artistic when in this area, thus I believe there lays the answer as to why I became the artist that I am. It is the same place that gave us the sculptors, John and Isaac Takawira, Bernard Manyandure, Jonathon Matimba, my poet cousins (David, Killian and Nicholas Mwanaka), the celebrated poet Musayemure Zimunya and many others.

It is not just for seeing how majestic the place is that I took this photo journey into the nearby hills. It is in fact the old civilisation that was there way before us the Bantu settlers that I am interested in. The evidence as to the evident existence of this civilisation is found in these small hills. I focus in on one of the hills and photograph the stone dwellings and shallow caves of this civilisation. The previous night I had asked my father about it. He doesn't know much about it. Maybe it's part of the larger Ziwa civilisation found to the south around Ziwa Mountain, which dates back to before 6th AD. These civilisations are older than the Great Zimbabwe. I would really like to investigate this further in the future, and so, I make a mental note to visit more hills with these dwellings of a long gone civilisation. I also take pictures of our rural burial grounds and the grave of my grandmother Helen, who died in 1989. I stayed with her in my teens so this journey to the graves is some sort of communion and connection. I am not scared a bit at this gravesite, considering my haunted, extracted feelings about these places I have expressed in several other writings before. I feel exercised a lot after this journey for I have sweated some, climbing the hill. I also take photos of the scrubby flowery and herbal plants, one of which I have uprooted for I want to plant it the far away in Chitungwiza.

The other facet of this old civilisation that I thought could help me document it were the big baobab trees that had been bored into, to create a dwelling home of sort inside its trunk, where I suppose these people would stay in as homes. There is no doubt these people were far short than us for the holes into the baobab tree were around half a metre to a metre long, and the caves in the mountains are shallow, and the entrance into these stone dwellings, in the above pic, as you can see, are short too. I remember some artworks I saw when growing up in one of the hills that I didn't visit in this excursion, were of drawings of little men and women, so my guess is this must be a Khoisan civilisation. Unfortunately the baobab trees I used to know with these dwellings, one of which was in our plot has erased this door by closing itself out to habitation. For some you can still see where the doors were but for a lot, it's fully closed. As the baobab expanded they closed off these doors (I want to think wounds). As the way a human being's wound heals.

I couldn't take the photos of the baobabs. I didn't feel the photos would explain the wounds to those who didn't see them when they were still an open wound and it felt like an invasion into the tree's private world now, just like we feel exposed when people see our unexposed wounds on our bodies. Every wound has a story, some are not so good.

7

Collectivism or Individualism?

The Western societies have moulded themselves, mostly around individualism, and most of the Third World (Non-Western) societies have moulded themselves around collectivism. For an example the African Bantu's philosophy was (is) "a person is a person because of others" (munhu munhu nevamwe/ abuntu abuntu ngabantu). The Western civilisation believed that the individual's freedom was more important than the society's wellbeing, thus an individual was allowed to shape the society more than the society was allowed to shape an individual. It was what they believed was correct and happening, but in actual essence, society would ultimately have a far-reaching effect on the individual. The collective effort and effects of the society is not an easy thing to shrug off. The problem with this individualism was a person would be allowed to selfishly pursue a lifeline, or goal, that would ultimately endanger the collective society like Hitlarian ideology that was well supported by the Germans during Nazi Germany. Non-Western society's emphasis on collectivism had its own problems. The problem of collectivism was it curbed on the ability of an individual to pursue society's enhancing dreams, thus it limited ambitions in the name of conformity.

The way to go now is where a society would allow both to flourish, each helping in shaping a balanced society. The days are long since gone where one person exists for himself or herself, and as well, where a society can be allowed to exert its limiting effects on an individual. An individual is part of the family cell, and a family cell is part of a community cell, and a community is part of a country.... I will resituate the bible story here, the metaphorical story about the body parts of a person. There are body parts like the hands, eyes, ears etc.... An eye is an eye, and it can only be an eye, and that is its individualism. No one can say it isn't an entity on its own. It sees what it wants to see, even though it sees what it has been directed to see by the other body parts. Its individualism is to see. It follows a hand is a hand, and an ear is an ear. All these are like people making up a society. So that a society can only be whole when all its parts work together for the better of the collective, so do the body parts. They need to work together.

It means we are part of the collective, even though we can be allowed to be whoever we want to be, and when our actions rapes and infringes on other people's well-being, we should try to moderate our ambitions so that they would help the society, especially in our quest of them. It should start with our thoughts- for they can shape our thinking, our actions, and our destiny. The biggest scourge of our uncontrolled individualism has now been seen with the perpetuation of corruption into our lives. This sore cancer has grown, and it's difficult to tame anymore. This has resulted in a small part of the population owning everything, the 99% versus 1% phenomenon we witnessed a few years ago. Even with all those demonstrations and the soul searching after, nothing has changed, yet. The thing with corruption is that once one gets hooked into it they don't know how else to stop it, like a drug abuse case. Drug users, once they get hooked into, let's say, cocaine, they would end up trying more and more intoxicating drugs. Their lives would become clotted into drug use. It is the same with corruption. A person's behaviour becomes changeable once he gets hooked into it.

When society has power over the individual, it allows the society to shape the actions of the individual, especially the dark excess of the soul to want to do wrong, to want to corrupt. Just as drug abusers are contained in the rehabilitation centre, and a process of rehabilitation is enforced, we need to step out of ourselves when we have lost our way too much, and get a better perspective of things, issues. We have to imagine ourselves as the collective; would we want us to hurt ourselves the way we have hurt others in this collective that we are. We see how much we represent the manifestation of a soul, we are the dreams that shape that soul, and thus our dreams become the beginning. Our dreams help us to shape us, thus they help us shape the society, so that collectively, we would face the event horizon, one way or another. The best way we would transcend this event horizon is for us to converge, to become one. We would become like the currency of electricity, whereby both wires (live, earth and neutral) are all important in carrying forward electricity to light a house. If we are to connect only one line, the live line, for instance, we won't get the flash, thus it means we won't get us. We are the flash, through our working together.

There is the telekinesis in us that allows us to link with the next person, thus we tape into the next energy field, in doing this we create excellences. Even the blessed trinity, God: The Father, God: The Son, God: the Holy Spirit works together as one entity to create us, to create masterpieces. So, we need to focus on each other, to touch one another, in creating better energy, better beings, and a better world. We have to continue improving ourselves. But in doing all this, as I have already noted, we still need our differences (individualism). These differences shape our search for perfection in us, in our collective society. We can't all conform and be zombies. What we need is a pin board where we all are allowed to pin our thoughts there. We allow each to help the other in continuously improving these thoughts that we have pinned on the board.

We have to adopt quality improvement cycles theory, of the Japanese Kaizen teams. Where a group would continuously (never ending) seek ways to improve the system, working together as a core group of employees. Thus we also have to allow the collective (family, cell, community, church, country) in us to shape us continuously. This openness will allow us to encourage curiosity as well as guard against the carnage of a bent mind, the dark excess of the soul to do wrong. It is us who created this bent mind, so it is our obligation to try to shape it. We can easily recognise it and its effects if we are open to each other, and start healing each other. When we can shape, or heal these destroyed minds, we also shape the future of our children, so that in them would not be found something damaging.

8

Desire and Passion

Desire. *n* . 1, a strong feeling of wanting to have something or wishing for something to happen. 2, strong sexual appetite. *Paperback Oxford English Dictionary*

Passion. *n.* 1, very strong emotion. 2, intense sexual love. 3, an intense enthusiasm for something. 4, Jesus' suffering and death on the cross. *Paperback Oxford English Dictionary*

"Desire names this place, possessive about panic." "A Streetcar Named Desire." These are statements I recall on desire. The first one is from my poem, *"Time"*. A play by *Tennessee Williams*, the second one needs no introduction. I desire you, desire; desire, desire… I desire to see the world, especially Eastern European cityscapes and scenery, but I don't love travelling. I want to be there without travelling. I don't desire, neither do I have a passion for travelling. I have a passion to write, that is a passion. For me to be able to write I don't just need to desire it, I need to have that strong emotion or love to want to write something, then I can write something. It would seem desire is less active than passion. Desire deals with feelings and passion deals with emotions, but they are interlinked. Desire starts, and the passion is the end.

Unfulfilled desire can be more lethal than passion because it can drive you for the rest of your life. It stays down there, becomes part of you, and continuously pushes the bad feelings up. Unfulfilled passion, especially when it's so hot, can make you implode. Then one can easily deal with the after-effects.

Desire has the problem of waylaying us into thinking we actually feel something for something when in actual fact we don't. We generally don't start the process of asking it, interrogating it, unless something moves us to do so.

Uninterrogated desire leaves you with nothing, when we lie to ourselves we have feelings for something that we don't have. Passion, generally speaking, as I have noted above, is always dangerous because it is always active.

Has anyone ever wanted something such that they feel lifeless when they don't have it? Have they ever wanted something to the extent that it becomes an obsession when they don't have it? Have they ever wanted something to the extent of the faith with which we all believe in and give allegiance to the almighty? It is a strange, yet also, a beautiful kind of wanting? Tendai Mwanaka, (unpublished novel) A Dark Energy.

This is passion, and it borders on the dangerous edge, it is bad passion for something. Yet the two, desire and passion, are very important to our lives. We need to have them, both balanced. It can be a desire or passion for anything, as long as you strike a balance. It could be desire or a passion for someone else, a project, and a place, a type of being or existence. The greatest passion of all should be the passion for your life. It is a few people who achieve on that. It comes from contemplating a lot about it. The process of contemplating about your life creates energy fields. Energy fields of passion, passion as a flow, a river, a movement. When it is flowing, when the river of passion is flowing, then you are immersed into the reality of your existence. Your mind and body will be aligned correctly, you will be focused.

I think we spent most of times trying to chase things that won't give us satisfaction. We are always attention deficiency people, such that we fail to create this energy that comes from genuinely trying to chase something that we are passionate about, that would give us satisfaction. Things that would make us feel we are a part of something larger than the reality of our existence. In pursuing these things we are not really passionate about we create lifetimes that are life-sentences. We serve time in our prisons. We feel stagnated.

We can always have desire or passion for something if we are always willing to learn. The more we want to know something, the more we become alive. I find it very fun when someone says he knows so much about something. We will never be able to know everything about anything. Even professors in a field of study don't know everything. The moment we say we know something is the moment we start dying, thus the need to continue learning, reading. Unfortunately a lot of people have stopped reading, thus have stopped learning. When we don't have passion or desire for something we are dead. Desire or passion is one tripod of life. The other two tripods are death and doubt. On these three legs a life becomes fulfilled. In this piece I will concentrate on passion, and will deal with the other two issues separately.

For a passion to become important in a person's life we need to trust it. For me to become a better and better writer, I need to trust I can write. I need to continuously trust I am writing something that I wanted to write, desired to write. Otherwise if I am forced to write about something I don't want to write about, I won't trust the passion in me. I won't write something that I would love. When we trust our passion it consumes us. It becomes an emotional workout, a hurricane of feelings. You find yourself being airlifted by it, consumed by it, immersed in it. You experience the freedom of a flying bird. You discover your secret depths. You are sinking into the ocean's bottom like a sea diver, but you still can breathe, thus you enjoy life down there. Your mind is alive, creatively alive and alert and the world around you is filled up with endless possibilities and wonder.

A passion can make you believe in yourself, you in the framework of this universe. As I have mentioned already, if passion doesn't feel right, as in the quote from my novel, *A Dark Energy*, above, it is now an obsession. Obsession is an addiction to passion and it is confusing and manipulative and doesn't create balance. Yes, an obsession can be good as long as we still have control over it, but it can be destructive when we lose control over it. It consumes us to destroy us, rather than to make us whole as the good passion would do.

Having a passion for something can make you create a difference in life. All that's required is for you to find what your passion is, then pursue and start making a difference. The difference starts on you, and as the light of your passion shines on you, you illuminate other people's lives. You give them the opportunity or possibilities of starting to believe in their own existences.

In order to discover your passion, you start at the base, which is trying to discover your desires. It is your desires, the feelings that provoke you to start thinking about something. Under these feelings, under these thoughts coming out from your feelings or desires, you will start finding your beliefs and convictions. It is below the convictions, behind developed convictions that you find yourself on your passions. It's a process that you have to carry out meticulously, and several times, until you are sure you have reached your passionate ground.

The passionate ground that is flowered with hope, fear, chaos, disorder, doubts… it is a Pandora box, a state of being.

Everyone has a Pandora box, but not everyone finds it in life. Those who find it won't usually stop from opening it. Already the journey to this point has made them so consumed with the want to do something, so they won't stop. Once you open this Pandora box, it is not easy to close it again. It's a fascinating world, of things we have stored deep down, in our secret places- dreams, hopes, fears etc. The biggest of which is fear. It is the biggest problem. If you let it predominate in this world, it would contaminate everything. Fear is both good and bad. Fear creates freedom, just like death. It maintains curiosity. Instead of curiosity kills the cat- when nothing else makes sense- curiosity keeps the cat alive. This is when fear is good; it keeps you on your toes. It is always good to look yourself squarely in the eyes and see who you truthfully are.

9

Death (Birth)

It might be in the morning, it might be in the afternoon, it might be at night, dawn, dusk... Someday, the event horizon is going to happen to me. Death is going to change this existence I have now into another. I can't think of this death as the opposite of life. Life doesn't have an opposite. Death is the opposite of birth. Just like I didn't have any control over my birth, I won't have any control over my death. These will just happen.

Death will just happen when it happens. There are no timetables, there are no choices, no when, how, where. It would just happen. These are the two things that would just happen to a person, death and birth. All the others, we can put some effort, or we can change our destinies. Birth and death happens, because as states of being, (or (not) being) we don't have any control over them. We can control the process of giving birth or of dying, but we can't control the states of birth and death. They are fraction-of-a-second happenings, and then we are in another life (or non-life).

So, if someone says love just happened to me, if someone says injury just happened to me, if someone says life is just happening to me, if someone says breathing, laughing, smiling is just happening to me, there are lying. These things, we can control (cause and effect) them. We make these to happen. One can always choose not to love, not to breath, not to get injured, most of the times. We never choose to enter the state of birth or death.

There is life before birth. It might even start before conception. The thinking that happens before sex (if there is thinking or discussions or agreements or arrangements, to try for a baby between two people), that's where life begins before birth. I did not put this argument to use on debates about abortion- whether it is killing or not. Up until birth, there is a life. Birth represents the death of that life, in giving birth to a new life. As I am writing this, I am living in a life after birth. There is going to be death, and then I would start living life after death. Maybe when we are on the other side we would call this death, a birth. I have always wondered what if some day humanity discovers a formula not to die. Then we should also discover a formula not to conceive and give birth, otherwise the earth wouldn't be able to accommodate all of us. Just think if every human being who has inhabited this earth, even those who died in birth, were inhabiting mother earth now, that is another 25 billion people, on top of the 7 billion we have now, the earth would be overwhelmed. So, death has acted as a natural process to create balance on this earth, so that normality will continue.

But, all the same, I would like not to die if I were given the opportunity. I think even the leaves on a tree do not want to die, to fall off the tree during the winters. It is a form of death for the leaves, so do some grass, animals... Even seasons die and new seasons come to impose themselves on us. With every life, when it dies it changes, just like the seasons. Each season comes different from the previous same season. We do the same. When we are not yet born, we are different from the way we are in life after birth, and when we die we will sure be different from now. The complex issue is to figure out whether after this death, there will be another one. Would we live in the life after death, for eternities? I am not talking about resurrection and life after resurrection for me, for all that is part of life after death.

So it means, if someone says you are dead- in thought, in life, in the heart, it should be an interesting preposition to explore. I would take it; I shouldn't feel they have insulted me. They mean; I am in life before birth or life after death, or getting into those lives. Since I am not in this life after birth they are working from, I have to be alive somewhere, and these are the only other places I could think of. In reality they are saying I have gone back to life before birth, since I was born, and they might be insulting me, yes. They are telling me that even though I might be alive in this life, I haven't been born to live the life I am alive in. This is too complex for someone to figure out whilst, at the same time, they are insulting you, and I wouldn't think they meant that. So, they meant the third alternative. If they are talking of life after death, or at that point of death, then I should feel honoured. It's obvious that even though they are thinking I am behind them, in actual fact, I am ahead of them. Rather, they should fancy me.

Growing up, trying to contemplate about death was something else. When I had figured out what death was all about, after witnessing the death of my brother, grandma, cousins, and many other relatives, I started obsessing about death. What I had realised was that they would never return back to be with me, again. I started obsessing about dying. Not mine, not yet. Even now I haven't started obsessing about death. I obsessed a lot about my parents' death. I think we are brought up to think they would die before us, so we just can't help it. Also, these represents the home we came from, and as people who are living away from their homes, we want to know whether these homes would still be there or not. It is total hell to obsess about all that.

I wanted to figure out how I would feel if they were to die, whom I would want to die first, father and mother. A lot people would say, father. I am sorry to all the fathers out there, I am also very sorry to the father inside me. I wouldn't want to be the first one. I also wanted to figure out what my life would be like after their deaths. Will I manage? I looked around me, at the families that had lost parents, and I didn't like it a bit. It obsessed me for years and years.

Deeper down, I had started developing my own death's obsessions, but they were in relation to one aspect, one illness. It wasn't about my death in general, which I have said, I don't obsess about. There is a time when a cousin died, cousin Charongwa. And we so loved him, that it just affected everyone badly. When anyone wants to be sad, to make everyone sad, even today, they remind themselves and others about this death. He died from liver cancer. It's the way he fought against it, how he suffered greatly, how he became helpless and hopeless. How we failed to secure finance for medication (chemotherapy) in South Africa. How it twisted the whole family, the fights, the disagreements....

This death obsessed me for years. It made me think of my own death, by cancer. I imagined all sorts of cancers infesting themselves on me without realising there were doing that to me. How even if I were to know about them, it was a hopeless situation. My life became a hopeless situation. This cousin died when he was around 35, and I always thought I won't go past that age. I was quite sure I was going to die before I reached 35. I think I put to hold a lot of things in life, always telling myself I shouldn't bother. I was dying. I would be dead by 35.

Now I am 40 years, and I now believe I am going to be around for some time. I don't obsess anymore about death, my death through cancer, or any other incurable diseases. I know it's going to happen someday. What I know is I have this now, and I am trying to live it, to revere it. Sometimes I see people of my own age starting to obsess about the ultimate event horizon, because they know they are ageing. I feel, I am glad; I did that possessiveness- about dying from cancers- a long time ago. It seems like it happened in another lifetime for me. I am not touched by it now. I am living life.

So, what are people afraid of, death or life? I would like to think they are afraid of life. That's what is there to think about. Death or birth are just small moments, the rest is life.

10

Doubt

Uncertainty with something is the driving force behind doubt. The thing could be familiar or strange- and it is difficult to differentiate what is what? It is the strangeness of a thing that makes me start doubting it, and in doubting it, I start the process of trying to understand it, to belong to it, or for it to belong to me. It is in my search for knowledge about something when doubt comes in. Not only knowledge in word image. Knowledge doesn't only reside in particulars.

All words are plastic beings being burned. Word images distort in the instant of utterance, thus it means knowledge works within a language group, outside of which, and it becomes irrelevant. Dangers even lurk in each system, through the unexamined beliefs of the creators of that system. It means, without trying to understand, or know about something- there is no doubt.

In pursuance of knowledge, there is that want for the knowledge to contain me into its meanings, and there is that part of me which wants to be thus contained. It is that part of me that does not want to be contained, that starts the doubting. Doubt in knowledge that I am acquiring is an important counter against conformity. It is the thinking, in the mind that refuses and refutes this knowledge, (sound, visual and textual) that asks questions as to whom I think I am looking at, and that inserts doubt. Doubt frames these questions. It is with doubt that borders of what is familiar (the truth) and what is strange (false) can be eroded. Doubt leaves me guessing, often uncertain, thus it drives me, it keeps me on the toes, in trying to figure out the truth. It leaves gaps, encourages me to find out more meanings, to doubt more, thus to acquire more knowledge (learning).

I always doubt a lot of things, some things other people would take for granted. I doubt love, myself, self, truth (that accepted as the truth), some spirituality aspects. There is pretty very little I don't doubt. I don't doubt that am alive. I don't doubt death. I don't doubt some of my desires to do some certain things. I don't doubt God. Why I can't doubt these entities or states is because I can't imagine a world where there are not there, that is; death, desire, God. I can't even begin to think, to doubt, that I am alive. This is one thing I believe without questions.

I know there are those who believe in a no-God universe (atheism) and those who believe in animals (American Indians animism), those who believe in scientology (self-knowledge and spirituality). Even though I don't believe in these non-God universes, I understand what they are about. They doubt the existence of the single God or multiple gods' world I am from. But, I even feel they believe in something (no-God, animals, knowledge), and these are their gods. So, if anything, I doubt them, from my side of the world, as well as they doubt my world.

The world I doubt a lot is love's worlds. It is always difficult to get head and tails of this issue. I want to love. I don't want to love. I don't want to love at my great expense, especially my (un-self) self's expense. I think a lot of it, what we are told is love, is more images and less substance. It seems love is more a sacrifice, an offering to unkind gods, a less sure thing or footing. For some, it becomes an apology. They are sorry life has failed them, or has failed those they loved. Some people, in fact a lot of people, stay in relationships they lie are love relationships, yet there are something else; pity maybe, imperfections, we can't think of our lives without these peoples. All these are things that drive my doubt. I doubt love, even though I would be crashing into it, even when I feel overwhelmed in feelings, emotions; even when my heart is breaking apart. I wrote these few lines about it, in the poem, *Why the giving proves mine alone*, in the poetry collection, *Playing to Love's Gallery, 2016*

> *She covers it, I wall it off, and then she hides it*
> *Tell me, why the giving proves mine alone?*
> *Like doubt to love to hate, hate to trust to dust*
> *And it would begin to doubt to love to hate*
> *And here is my love-mirror, a sweet see*

Doubt in my "self"; it would seem, it is in my longing (public longing and secret desire) for wholeness in which misunderstandings of self and origin happens. Who am I? Who are you? Where did I come from? In the absurdity of the cultural flux that I now live in, questions of where I am from are difficult to answer. *Judith Butler, 2004*, offers the undoing of self through the telling of a story in, *Undoing Gender*, saying, the very I, which seeks to tell the story, should be stopped in the midst of telling. That through it all I am undone, so that what I am told (not what I want to tell) undermines what I see.

Generally, the mind want to impose this framework it calls reality- this framework is independent of what my senses have reported. To counter this, the emphasis would now be on experience, not on knowing. Then doubt comes in on self and identity. If self is not fixed, is in multiple selves, if self is performed; then identity is not about origin or colour. Self becomes ephemera withering in the blaze of the unknown, infinity. I am formed through discourse; through interactions with others, the environment etc..; and that is a shifting world, thus I become unfixed, in trying to fix myself somewhere. Self and origin becomes unfixed, as well. This is my very agency; curtailed through fixing, lost through a complete unfixing.

Another way to exercise doubt is to infiltrate into those strange and familiar places, inserting myself as part of them, and then doubt from the inside. I don't doubt from the outside, that I would do when I am acquiring knowledge. I do that, mostly, with spirituality worlds. I doubt it from the inside, rather than from the outside. Generally religion oppresses curiosity, and the only way one can get this knowledge is to get inside, and doubt from that inside. It would be a true visionary, or prophet, that would stand in the presence of God, with the full knowledge of where he stands. This doubting from the inside creates an energy field uncaring of anything, except as of creation, which is what visionary ecstasy should be about. I am a prophet, and somewhat, it gives me the right to participate in my life, in my existence.

It is the dialect of experience and interpretation that Nikki S Lea and Miwon Kwon argue for. In the inside, one is confronted with evidence and disjunctions- what I see and what I am told. Multiple selves acknowledge the coercive nature of cultural norms of performativity. It signals, on one hand, the desire to choose for oneself what to look like, whilst on the other hand, it is a whimsical fashioning out of what ifs I have to experiment with. Butler, 2004, says,

> If I have an agency, it is opened up by the fact that I am constituted by a social world I never chose. That my agency is riven with paradox does not mean it is impossible. It means only that paradox is the condition of its possibility.

She says, it's in our undoing that new possibilities would arise.

When I was 14, in grade seven, we were a day before writing our primary education qualifying exams. It was Sunday, and in that Sunday I woke up feeling something bad was going to happen to me. It was just this instinctual feeling I had. I knew it deep down my bones. My brother told me we should go fishing and I said, no. I didn't want to go. He pushed it. He assuaged me, he begged me, and he wore me down. Back then, if he did that, I could be swayed from my instincts. So, eventually, I accepted to go with him, fishing.

We were digging for worms in a swamp close to the river, to use as bait, when I was bitten by those big blackish-brown wasps, on my eyes, on my face. We run for cover, and later went to the river to start fishing. But I was paining all over my face, like hell. When we got to the river, I was almost beaten by three snakes that had surrounded me. Bernard had to help me beat them off, before they beat me. I wasn't seeing much by that time, my face was swelling vastly. That day we didn't catch any fish, and hell, not even a tadpole. By the time we got home my face was a swollen melon. The morrow day I went to school to take my exams.

That day, I wrote the English exams swollen. Other kids laughed at me. I had to peel or raise the upper eye lip so that I could see, read the questions, think about the answers, raise it again as I marked the right answers, so that I didn't finish the exam, thus I got the 4th grading in this subject. When I wrote Maths, two days later, I was seeing well, as the swelling had subsided. I got the 1st grading in Maths, the best grading for the entire school, for that subject. This episode always reminded me of the consequences of doubting your inner impulses or instinct, even further, of how to doubt the doubting process, itself. I doubted what my whole body was telling me, and thus I learned a hard life lesson through that, through doubting the self. There are many other instances, later in life, when I doubted myself, and it was always with consequences, but I couldn't have done otherwise. It's part of me, the doubter in me.

11

Dear John

It is very difficult to talk about it, John. But, I am your Auntie, your father's sister, so I will try. I know your father will never discuss this with you. It is taboo in our culture. Your mother won't talk about it. This is where I come in. Don't say, 'no' to Auntie Dotty. I am going to talk to you about sex.

I know your mind has jerked up. Everyone wants to hear about this. It's a demesne of fantasy and fabrication. Have you ever seen even how trees and flowers bloom well, when they are preparing to attract each other, have you seen how the roster and hen play at it, have you ever realised how confounding the fish' world is, how about the people, the animals... Sex has always been a word that would make people shy and fearful, even these days, when it is all over. It is big business, but it is still difficult to talk about it. I would also want to run a parallel with the Don Juan personality, that I think you are, John. You have remained an outsider to your sexual life.

They say the wolf comes from the Stone Age and, it still is here with us. It is everywhere now, that it is difficult to differentiate who is not and who is. Sex is now a game. They (I mean you, boy or girl) now lead a life of misspent young adulthood of sex, drugs and hip-hop, rock and roll, the pop culture; littering the towns with off-springs they would refuse to acknowledge. How many kids do you have out there, John. Many; don't even think to start counting. How many of these girls have you married, telling them you will be there through thick and thin for them and that you will be there for your children. But your unsavoury paraphallic obsessions, particularly your hunt of sex, affected your own children, found you being quickly demoted to persona-non-grata by these girls and your own children.

I want you to un-separate between sex and love, John. I know the young girls are so tight-kerned and you feel like you could pry a needle from their tight-asses, with your tractor, but those of our fairer sex mix the two; sex and love. I am sure you tell yourself that sex and love are two different things, otherwise there is no fun in the game. A boy can shack everywhere, every time, but is that love. Maybe, it is. I will start on the Cape floral kingdom. It is a place somewhere on the southern tip of Africa. It is a place abundant with flowers, which bloom through the year. I am sure you are asking me where the hell I am bitchiking off to with this story. Be patient, young man.

You can see how the bees carry pollen from one flower to another in the Cape. No, they are not having it. Theirs is the search of food, their own food, their own nectar. It's the trees that they will be helping populating, and inversely their world, as well. It's in the corks of honey where the queen bee finds its womb for her eggs. Is that sex, you are asking me. There is no one flower dicking into the other, you ask me. It is a dull way to perpetuate, I am sure you are telling me that, too. Where is the fun? But if the trees and flowers bloom and look lovely, and if the trees and flowers feel they are having a great time, I suppose it must be fun (sex), ummm. Someday, if the trees were to get a good handle of a book that deals with this issue, I am sure there is going to be mighty little pollen-totting done by the bees. And, you think why they just fucking don't extrude the bees out of the equation if they want to have it, by doing it through their roots. It might be funny and interesting; a very private affair, I agree with you, nephew. No one would know what's happening down there, in terra land. It might teach a lesson or two to the wolf personality in you, John. You don't have to shout, at the top of your voice, about it; no kissing and no telling, nephew. There is nothing to boast about it. Hell, you are not Adam, making everything new.

Remember, in your late teens, you were like that artist *prince* or *simple* or whatever he is now; you started calling yourself, HIM (! ~ `@*#$$ %&&**), an image which was irksome, it was unpronounceable, so you resorted to writing it down on the paper for us. You were boasting of your image, you as a sex symbol. And a couple more years you had changed your image into HE (**&& %$$^^*#@!~~), like those boy band lookalikes, it was difficult to figure out the differences. You had a greater range of expressions than the additions of motion, sound and lighting all added together, could afford. You worked on your skin, tattooing on it whirling tribal patterns. Nehanda's colours; you lied to those with traditional sense of identity. Flowing sickles and curlicues to mask the bland smooth lines you always found staring back at you in the mirror. And you could lie to those who didn't decipher it that it was Japanese for "I love my mother". The mother you didn't even love. Every pattern is different from the other, John. But, a cold heart is bland and patternless.

A normal tree doesn't holler at every other tree, doesn't overdress itself, doesn't talk to every tree, as if she were a possible bed companion, doesn't flash the, "look, I am a man" signal. If they did, I am sure the Cape floral kingdom would be inaccessible for the likes of us. We now come to China. Or rather let's explore South Africa, a bit before we take our flight to China. On the northern fringes of South Africa, yes, in Kruger National Park in South Africa, or Gonarezhou

National Park in Zimbabwe, or even Limpopo National Park in Mozambique, together it is now known as Great Limpopo Transfrontier Park. It's the biggest park in the world. Where is the lesson, you ask me? It is the same, as with all the other animals, as it is with us. There is a lot of courting, kissing, dating, paying of lobola, marriages, adultery, sex...everything, nephew. I am interested in the duck, in the banks of Limpopo River, John. Take a look at its eggs. Duck's eggs! They are not when they are at the grocery shop. They are now the grocer's eggs. Ask him, if you think I am lying, "how much are your eggs", and he will reply you confidently, "dollar for six". They are almost round, but not quite. Are human eggs the shape of duck's eggs?

Hen's eggs! Surely they are from the hen. When you buy them, there are now your eggs; there are no longer a hen's eggs, neither the grocer's eggs. But you should know a red cocked rooster had sex, for you to have your own eggs. It had to deal with the dating game, the courting, the chasing... Once it got its sex, it didn't care, only about having more sex.... It's not the Don Juan personality, as such, nephew. It is controlled sex. Remember it had to dupe the hen, for the ulterior good of its species, so that you would also have your eggs. Remember, it has a red crest on top of its head. A hen can see it kilometres away and alight from the taxi, or make previous engagements stand. It could even work out a headache, but the stubborn roaster would be patient. Chase the hen until it has its sex, your sex for you to have your eggs, or roasted chicken meat. Don't just have your sex, young man. You should know that God created sex as the greatest instrument for human connection and perpetuation. That's why the Church wants to control it, as well. The church, I won't try to talk about it. Don't say, "Stop now, Auntie Dotty". I am not going to talk about that.

But, John, do you know that your hit and run behaviour, is now a nuisance to society. It is leaving a train of unhappiness and bitterness, John. It can only be the work of a low sexual appetite person, John. You are warring with yourself, nephew. I know my sister-in-law; your mother- was your favourite person when growing up. You had no connection with your father, my own brother. You still don't have any relationship with him. Your mother's favouritism of you, nephew, and your father's disapproval are the prime reasons you are like that. You mother was the one who was always explaining you to your father, so you turned to your mother.

Colours have a tendency to do the same, too. I am sure you are wondering whether I am still talking about sex here. Yes. When we mix colours, we are like the bees carrying pollen from one tree to another, pollinating. Don't gag! It is not semen dripping down your hands. It is paint, John. When we mix black and white we get grey. It is sex of colours, nephew. It is safe, though, to say you enjoy painting, young man. You are just a vessel. Sex psychologists must be agreeing to this, just as they believe when you displace sex into pain, in your sex escapades, it is not your fault. Hate hates the hater more than it does to the object of hate. You long for your father's esteem, so you will be transferring this longing into a *hate and love* relationship with the female species. It's your mother, in your mind, who is responsible for the withdrawing of the father's approval. Don't ask me how come you blame your father. You do, nephew. It's your father you want to destroy, in your mind, in your eyes, so you are an individual perpetuating this hate, and you feel so inadequate, that you can't rest until the object of hate is destroyed, and in the process you are destroying yourself. You now seek your father's approval in every woman, every mother you try to destroy. It is all about doubt of mother's love and approval, and father's disapproval, which is making you do that. You doubt every woman; you don't respect women, or like them, so you use them. There are your allies- mercenary troops to help you fight off the masculinity world your father represents, so you despise yourself for engaging them. Your interest in a woman declines steeply with the first touch, making it difficult to stand up for what women mean. This brings me to the Australian Great Barrier Reef area. Yes somewhere, there in the bowels of the south pacific. It is a beautiful fish world, out there, nephew.

Fish are probably the worst example of the wolfian personality, you could ever find anywhere. For starters, they work under water so the positions must be difficult to achieve. You won't find one fish in a million that has enough sense to come in when it rains. Stupid, that's all they are, especially in their sex life. Take, for instance, a female Carp fish; it finds it impossible to live with any men fish, but it also has to do its job. It knows it's impossible to perpetuate without the male carp fish. It has very little forehead, and generally brings nothing to the conversation. Let's say, some fine spring morning, the mother carp has decided it wants to have children. Just like that. No discussion with father, no preparation, no worries, no pregnancy, and I know I am talking of some of those girls you use... So, she would take a deposit slip and deposit a cool million dollars, I mean eggs, nephew, on the rocks, on the reef; a cool one million dollars somewhere in the Cayman Islands, Panama or in the revered Swiss banks. Once this is accomplished, it dusts its small forehead, powder its nose, and swims away, like a woman with a past. You do the same with the young ladies who are attracted to your Don Juan personality, nephew. These young women will be thinking it's the old script they are reading from. Marriage! Once you are done with a woman, you brag a bit about your conquests, and your brags are soulless, so empty like a city abandoned by any kind of light. And then, you leave the young lady to find her way. That's what the mother carp would do to its eggs.

Then, in comes papa carp into the picture. Papa's job is very casual. He swims over a million dollars, and takes a chance that by sheer force of his personality; he can induce half a dozen of them to hatch out. The remainder goes to waste, or they make your caviar, nephew. Caviar and wine, yes, young man, it's like your duck's eggs. So you see that the sex life of a fish will represent what your sex will eventually be. You will despise yourself; you will grow sadder and never would understand women and love them. Feigning ignorance, of the teenage pretences, of not knowing what you are doing to yourself and to these girls, while the extravasations continue unabated. Fish don't understand love, oh I mean, sex. At least in their world, there are no committees set up to regulate it.

I won't delve into the unicellular organisms, nephew. Those that reproduce by dividing themselves into twos, fours, eights, etc...., as you can see, there is no lesson in that. The math doesn't just compute, nephew. One plus one is two, isn't it? There is nothing to refute here. So take that flight to China, nephew. It has been hanging on your head for far too long. China has the biggest population of any country on mother earth, Nephew. It's all about sex. I can feel it on every Chinese face. I know Japan might say we have better statistic; in terms of per square kilometre. India might come in, arguing on another platform. I am not arguing. Yes, you are correct to go anywhere South East Asia, nephew. I won't delve into the reason, why in Asia. It must be because of the religions most dominant in Asia versus those that are most dominant, in say, the Western World, Africa, Americas. Control of church over sex, nephew, I have said too much already. Just know that there is no such thing as a hundred percent female, or a hundred percent man. I am sorry it is going to throw a lot of people out of work, but think of the heartaches it would save you, and the money. Now you know, nephew.

So, think this issue through carefully now. If you let someone use your body for their own gratification, and if you use your body for your selfish gratification, you are responsible for the damage done to your psyche, so also, their psyches. You cannot escape your psyche, nephew. So, keep the sex clean, nephew. Take the nearest exit from being a wannabe man, by making a detour into being the grown up that you ought to be, John.

My name is Auntie Dorothy, and I thought of writing this letter to John, my nephew, after reading some hieroglyphic Pangaean extracts of this issue in the Lilliput magazines of the mid twentieth century muddies.

12

It's Not about Me: Dairies (2010-2011)

It's a Thursday today. I have nothing against Thursdays; I have never had any issues about Thursdays, maybe Mondays. Manic Mondays!

Thursday, December 16, 2010

It's the heat, hot, sweltering heat. It's so hot. It's in the morning, but as hot as any summer afternoon. I take a pair of my shoes; one of leather, another sneakers, to the cobbler at Zengeza 2 Shopping Centre. I have to suck up to the smell of the nearby stinking Council toilet, as I wait whilst he is doing the shoes. These toilets are always that dirty, with urine and faeces all over the place. You have to be that desperate or brave to use them. On the way, I meet some girl. Nothing worth talking about this girl, she is a street girl but a bit on the loose. She has had love, sex, marriage escapades, one after another. Back, in 2006, she was barely thirteen or fourteen; she once offered herself to me. She kissed me, but I couldn't take her on. She simply was too young for me. Now, I wasn't taking it for anything. She is rather clinging for my liking.

The cobbler looks so old and worn down by life, by the Nipper concoction he guzzles. It's some white spirit beer (Nipper) which he is constantly consuming. You can even use this beer as a substitute for paraffin, for it burns some. He is mixing it with water, which is cheaper to get, at a local tape, than drinks which are expensive. He is talking, mostly gibberish, as he works on my shoes. I can only grunt replies to him or just being silent so as not to encourage him. I can be so dump, so bored when I want to discourage people, people who are talking machines, boring talking machines. Why should I suffer them? Eventually he stops trying to talk to me. It has always been difficult for me to try to maintain conversation with a drunken person. I usually run away.

I remember some time I was staying with my brother in South Africa, in 2008. He was a drunk, he still is. When he was so drunk, he would return home in the early hours of morning, and he would come to my room and try to strike conversations, at one or two in the morning. You should know how painful that can be. In the first days I used to tolerate him, even when everyone else in the house was awake, they feigned to be dead asleep, so that they wouldn't encourage him to talk to them. Even his wife would feign to be asleep. My brother is very argumentative and quarrelsome when he is drunk, and I took it well, until I started feigning to be asleep, as well; when he arrives late nights or early mornings. Talking to someone drunk, has always made me feel I was talking to myself, or that they would just as well be talking to themselves. They don't really care about what you think, don't even listen to you, but they want you to listen to them; as if the beer has clothed them with the wisdom of Solomon they were lacking without the beer. It is "Dutch Courage", after all!

Not that the cobbler was doing such a great job on the shoes as such, no. I didn't really mind losing the fiver for this patch up job; at least he didn't destroy them, so I can always have them redone by someone else. I made the mistake of approaching him in the first place. I am paying the consequences of such a rush decision. I should have consulted with other people for the best cobbler there was at the shops. There are definitely other better cobblers.

*****

I have called my cousin, Bernard, around the afternoons. In our culture and language we call him an uncle, but in English it's a cousin. His father and my mother are siblings. I phoned him about my application materials that I had sent through with South African bound buses. I couldn't talk to him because he was asleep from his night shifts. I thought sending my application through with the buses, for them to be posted in South Africa, was the best way to get the things through before deadline day. He will be posting them for me in South Africa. Not only because of that alone. Yesterday, when I was preparing the materials, I checked with my local post office at our local shops, Zengeza 2 Shopping Centre. The teller, in his late twenties, admitted that the post office was still opening letters before posting them to outside destinations; so that the politicos would know who was disseminating bad stuff about the government and the country. Anything critical of the government, or country was viewed as bad for the country by the politicos, would land you in hot soup. Considering that my application stuff was inflammatory, political, and very much against the entity here, I thought I could save myself from heartache buy not using the post here. It simply was survival instinct.

*****

Uncle Bernard called me a couple of hours ago telling me that the bus driver whom I had entrusted with my application stuff had demanded for some more drink money for the materials from him. It is just after midday, around two. The suck thing is that I had paid that pig of a driver some drink monies already for the parcel here. So, I am going to have to pay twice now. It's very expensive, the total costs of getting the stuff to its destination, in Germany (DAAD fellowship), considering I still have to pay for the postage in South Africa, but it's a price I am prepared to pay, in exchange for my safety

*****

As the afternoon dredges the day into the evenings, the noise in the streets has increased. I am trying to adapt to so much noise, so many sensations, and so much life at the grunt level. It's so visceral. Svosve Street, our road, has always been like that. So noisy, so full of life; it's sometimes so overwhelming, but I know I will get used to that sooner. After all it has been my home for as long as I know. 17 plus years I have stayed here permanently, since I finished my 'A' levels, about 1994. It's a long time ago. Sometimes I wonder what has happened to all this time, to me, to a lot of things. But the noise in Svosve Street stops you from wondering too much.

There is noise of little boys and girls playing in the streets. I used to be part of that world. It's so loud. Was I that loud, I know I was? It's as if they are aware very soon it will be dark; so they have to make the very best use of the few hours left of the day. There are also old people calling each other, exchanging greetings, their laughter; the honking of car horns; the drowning sounds of aircraft passing on top of me; the blaring sounds of high volumes radios. I have taken so easily to my old vice, that of playing my radio at the highest decibel level; so as to blot out any other noise. As long as it's not music, it disturbs me. So, I let the music create the conducive atmosphere for me to do the writing, the thinking. I am getting used to working daily on my craft despite all these other sensations fighting for my attention.

Friday, December 17, 2010

Today, I also met a very close old friend that I hadn't seen in over two years. He came over by my place. It was so sweet and emotional to see him again. It's a real homecoming treat for me. He has been married for some couple of years. I had heard some stories when I arrived; that they had been having problems in their marriage, and that, the wife had had extra marital affairs. I don't know what I would do if my own wife would have that. I will lose it, I am sure of this. But, it's something that I couldn't ask him. I tend not to really like getting involved or even getting to know stuff like that, especially between people who were married. It's a minefield because at the end, if you get involved, and you had given some advice, you would be left feeling like shit and stupid, especially when they get back on good terms and your advice hadn't encouraged that. I would rather people who are in a relationship should sort their own problems, on their own, without involving others. So I tried not to get involved in his problems, if there were still there. I didn't even ask him about that. My sister Judith did that. She is a bit nosy, like all women are. He told her the problems were not of infidelity, as she had heard, but just silly problems that had now been sorted.

Tuesday, December 21, 2010:
Chitungwiza Mushamukuru (large village).

It sprawls, unobtrusively, for kilometres on end, north-south, west-east, not much upwards, not much downwards.

Chitungwiza Mushamukuru, of dunk atmospherics. Chitungwiza Mushamukuru, affectionately known as Chi-Town by its inhabitants, of ragged, potholed roads and streets, you could even go fishing in the streets. Chi-Town Mushamukuru, of boxed-up, small Bronx-like houses, like matchboxes. Chitungwiza Mushamukuru, of an endless chatter, clatter, cacophony, radios and music blasting at high volumes; for it is always a party thing in Chi-Town! Chitungwiza Mushamukuru, a cloth for the poor; you still cloth them decently. Chi-Town Mushamukuru, you have survived the scourges of the last two decades, always bustling with humanity. Humanity clothed in patience, determination; it's a determination to face life every day. Laughing, smiling, crying, but still facing life bravely. Chitungwiza Mushamukuru, I love you like a second wife. I was not born here, but I gave birth to myself here. Chi-Town of beautiful flowers; marsh's flowers, cobbled stone's flowers, dusty fields flowers, dusty roads flowers, tarred roads' flowers, flowers that can withstand anything. Chitungwiza Mushamukuru of young and old man who should have given up on life; but are still waking up every day, believing that they could earn something out of their despondent situation, and lives. Chi-Town Mushamukuru, of young women, of old women who still carry on as if nothing was the matter with their lives, offering that sweet love and warmth to their little boys, little girls, big girls, big boys, young man and old man- pushing this pregnant humanity into life, with their love.

*****

Maybe I am beginning to like it here, that's why I wrote that praise poetry, dairy, or whatever it is above. It reminded me of poetry of the Negritude school; Langston Hughes, Senghor, etc....I don't usually like to write stuff like that, praising things, trying to relate to things through praising them. It should just happen without trying to put it into words. Some years ago, a certain poetry editor tried to describe me, my poetry, said it is of this Negritude school. Maybe just because I am black! I don't feel any connection to this school, just like I don't feel any connection to any other school. Yes, I respect a lot of schools or establishments out there, but I simply write, as best as I could. I don't try to define myself according to any constructs.

Wednesday, December 22, 2010

Whilst I am writing this piece I am listening to Susan Howe interviewing Charles Bernstein (American poet/professor) and Bruce Andrews (American poet/professor of politics at Fordham University). They are talking poetry, writing, language..., especially about language. They are talking of their magazine, The Language Magazine. Bruce read his poems "How", and "RNB." My mind prickles on what he is bumbling grinding about, so much verbosity, and such attitude! It's American, I think. I am feeling stunted in my creativity. They are talking and they are saying writing has lagged behind all the other creative arts, especially poetry. "Is it lagging or dying?" Well there are talking and they are in the 70s so maybe they are correct in saying lagging behind. They say poetry doesn't produce instant gratifications that say visual art produces on the consumer. When you look at the words of a poem they are just words, strewn haphazardly on the page. They are saying you have to read it several times for you to start feeling into it. They are saying it is for this that it has lagged behind. That society is generally geared toward consumptive arts.

At one time Charles coughs whilst getting into the drifts of his philosophical, linguistic discourses. It halts my thinking and it gets me thinking. "Is he coughing now, does his coughing embodies the now their work or beliefs have already done with me?" To me coughing, like laughing, or even talking, without reason or ambition have always been things I thought would disappear into the thin blue air. If you don't record them you won't hear them again. You can't get them back, but maybe the feelings, or memory of what they made you feel like when you heard them. But the coughing in this reading seems to be happening today as I listen to the reading, yet he did coughed in the late 70s. Then Charles read his long poem, "Matters of policy." I love Charles hands down. He is such a great writer and performer of his work and he creates fantastic music with his reading. I am now very much alive as I drift with Bernstein.

Thursday, December 23, 2010

It's been one heck of (almost) three weeks now. I came into the country on 4 December, and I have been around for slightly over two weeks. This I realised last night. I am overwhelmed, seeing people I hadn't seen for over two years, seeing what change has done to them, to me too, the emotionality of it all! It's as if you can just rewind time, just for a moment and relive things all over again, but you also know that you can't do that. Another thing I seem to be grappling with; is knowing and dealing with the fact that time really, actually moves on. People die, marry, divorce, and disappear without a trace…. It hits me in a kind of big way that I seem like grounded fish because I haven't done any of the above. I had moved on, or out with my life, but I am back. It's tough to know that whilst others cannot go back, I can still go back. That's what I am thinking; it is the only way I can connect with something of my past, which isn't even there in the first place! So, I don't connect to anything. I feel lost and grounded. Maybe it's a passing moment; maybe I will eventually find something...

The other thing is trying to reach out for friendship. There are a lot of friends I could reach out to. I could make new friends. I could even close some unfinished chapters, that have needed closure, but all that are boggling prospects with me. Maybe it's because I am expecting too much from me, from them, from life. I have been leading a hermitical life, for the most part of those two or so years; and somehow it seems I can't shake it off.

*****

I am reading Emmanuel Ngara's poetry collection, "Songs from the Temple." I have bought it as a gift for a friend, Juanita Torrence Thompson. She is the editor of *Mobius Poetry Magazine*, New York. She has published my work twice now. It's the last poems in this collection, "Songs from the Temple," that captures me. Temple, is the temple Zimbabwe? The Songs must be painful, sorrowful; angry songs. Zimbabwe has this ability, of evoking such feelings because life here is always visceral and painful. The first batches are revolutionary rhetoric, though they are particular ones that deal with the bombings of Nyadzonya, Chimoi, and Tembwe, the killings of the liberators during the liberation war in the 70s, which are worth commending.

For some days I have been visiting bookshops in Harare and Chitungwiza looking for the right collection to give this friend. Altogether I have counted only 4-5 collections in the bookshops I have visited, most of which were published over

2 decades ago. There is no doubt there is death of literature in the country, evidently seen by the closure of, for instance, Kingstons Book Shop in Chitungwiza, the only book shop in Chitungwiza at that! Those branches of Kingstons that are still functioning in Harare; there is not much new stuff in these bookshops. Another facet is all the collections are politically correct, and are in praise of the regime in Harare, not in exception is Ngara's collection. That's so defeating!

Saturday, December 25, 2010

I am staying alone again. It seems like it's my perpetual condition, having flirting touches for human contact. I returned back from South Africa where I had stayed for nearly 2 years of the 2, 5 years alone, to crash into our family home where my sister was staying. We have stayed together for a collective three weeks, and now she is moving on. She got remarried. When I was getting used to staying with someone again, all of a sudden I am alone again and it's on Christmas day. Off course, its lonesome but one sometimes gets used to the situation. So I am not going to whine a lot. Life moves on, has to move on, and its normal I think; to feel sometimes left out. It shows you still want to be part of something, somehow. But you can't also help noticing that the biggest part of you feels like some museum piece- completely left behind. Your life; those parts that are a relic watches life, the rest of your life passing by you. There is still, though, that want to grab things, to own them and its sweet to know that.

25th of December has come up again, Christmas! You have stopped colleting, how many times it has come up, though. It is no longer an event, even though you see some people trying too harder to make it feel like it is something. It doesn't do that for you. It is like any other day, so you look at it with the same disposition, the one you have used for years to delve into a day.

Twenty fifth of December, it is so hot. I even feel the heat coming out of my nostrils, mouth and skin pores. My body is caked in sweat and it seems as if I am being roasted slowly on low heat coals....

Thursdays, September 1, 2011

I am getting into my 10th month since I returned back from South Africa. You don't get to do things easily here, even writing, but you have to keep focused, trying. I am absorbed into the editing of KEYS IN THE RIVER. She is a great editor I am working with, Jennie Oliver, I am beginning to realise this. She is very helpful, yet not intrusive. I have always thought working with a woman editor is a great thing. Why? Because I feel I write from the heart, like a woman. I tend to flow gently with my writing so it's a blessing to be working with Jennie Oliver. She didn't disappoint my expectations. There is a bit of work to be done, it seems. I am focused on that.

Saturday, September 3, 2011

I can't help revisiting a story I wrote, a couple of weeks ago, in these diaries, about Mujuru's death. It's a mysterious death, definitely. Nobody, up to now, has been able to explain how someone could burn to the extent of beyond recognition, to the extent of his remains failing to fill up a plastic bag. We were talking about this with my friends, Pardon and Nikki Mlambo (they are brothers). I haven't been following the issue for some time now, but after hearing the wife of Solomon Mujuru, Vice President Joyce Mujuru, talking about it on the Tele, a couple of days ago, has raised my interest again. She was saying she is still waiting for answers, and that none have been forthcoming. Also after seeing a title in the independent newspapers saying that the death was mysterious, I am beginning to get absorbed into it like the whole nation at large. Everyone is waiting for an explanation.

It reminded me of 3 years ago, in the March 2008 election period when the whole nation waited with bathed breath for the election results, how the waiting was both intriguing and confounding, and the stories that abounded, then. It is the same situation now. It is said in some of the stories that Mujuru was drunk, he came home, at his farm in the Beatrice area, alone. His electricity is directly connected to the main grid and that the electricity doesn't go out at his farm, like it doesn't go out on the president and government minister's residencies. They have a separate line straight from Kariba. Some people are saying the electricity cables had been cut from the grid so that his place was in darkness when he arrived drunk. The generator hadn't been connected, or that it hadn't automatically connected to generate electricity, which is curious. Despite the fact that he is guarded, 50 metres from the residency, by the police, nobody came into the home with him. He entered his residency with his pistol; bar the grocery he had left in the car, had collected the keys from his workers. It's suspicious nobody, not even the police and his workers thought that he deserved protection or help in such a situation. He entered the house alone. He was burned to death. The source of the fire is still a mystery, and despite the fact that his bedroom, which is on the first floor, with three outlets (doors), unlocked, with no burglar bars on the windows, huge windows, yet he couldn't just walk out of the fire. He had to be incapacitated that badly (comatose) for him not to get out of the house; even beer was not good enough to incapacitate him that way. The mystery is why someone as strong as he was, who was remotely drunk, could be burned to death, to nonentity from a fire supposedly started by a candle with all those possible escape roots, with also the security details not more than 50 metres away. How could a candle light burn someone to death and how such a fire could burn down a fire proof building to that extend? The previous owner, a white commercial farmer, who had arrived a couple of days from outside the country, confessed the building was fireproof. How could a candle fire destroy it? This farm, it seems, Mujuru was occupying it illegally.

Speculation has been rife that it is a politically motivated killing, some saying he was killed by a petrol bomb, some saying he was already dead by the time he entered the building from gunshots, some even saying that that's some mad man they killed in the place of Mujuru, and that Mujuru is somewhere in Asia, enjoying his life out there and having the last laugh at ZANU-PF's power games. Nobody will know for sure who died in that inferno, how he was killed, who is responsible. Like the whole nation, I am gripped, enthralled by this. I want to know the explanations; maybe we will have to wait for more than the month we waited for the election result in March 2008, to know for sure what happened. The most likely thing is it's going to be another unexplained happening, like the other killings before him. At least this time there have created another storyline...*Burned to death*. We were now tired of the road accidents, the Army Puma vehicles creating the soaps for us...

I would like to penetrate into this new storyline but the unfortunate thing is there is too much loose ends...a lot of unexplained parts, and it's fascinating and confounding at the same time. Some other people are already convinced it is the work of Mugabe. That he wanted Mujuru out of the way, that

Mujuru has always been a constant thorn in Mugabe's flesh, that Mujuru was opposed to early elections, that Mujuru, in the Wiki-leaks cables, was holding meetings with the United states ambassador on successor strategies, that Mujuru even supported Simba Makoni in the last election, at least for some time until Mugabe stringed him into line. Some saying Mujuru was going to benefit from the election delay..., that is if Mugabe dies before the elections, automatically the wife of Mujuru would be the head of state, without having to contest against the old man at ZANU-PF, or even through the election route, thus Mujuru would benefit, his businesses would grow better.

The Mnangagwa camp is going to get on the wrong end of this situation. He is the obvious suspect for everyone else. Since he is a bit down in the ZANU-PF's hierarchy he will have little chance to benefit from both situations now. Either, the two, Mnangagwa and Mugabe had a good motive to want to see the back of the general, the kingmaker, but all in all, it is anyone's guess on who did it. We most likely will never get to the bottom of this. We have never got to the bottom of the other many political killings before so it's going to be a hard fruitless wait.

Tuesday, September 13, 2011

The political situation here is becoming slippery. The wiki-leaks are setting the tone here. There is some hullaballoo as the ZANU-PF hierarchy were said to have had secret meetings with the USA ambassadors (Dell, McGee, Sullivan), not to mention Ray Charles, the present USA ambassador. The ZANU-PF bigwigs fingered include the Vice President Mujuru, Vice President Joseph Nkomo, Simon Khaya Moyo (National Chairman of ZANU-PF). Minister Savious

Kasukuwere, the indigenisation minister who is being vilified over the mining and industrial indigenisation programme, Reserve Bank governor Gideon Gono, who is said to have confided with USA ambassador Christopher Dell, saying he had resigned, on 6 august 2006 as the governor, but was forced back into the job by the presidium and Didymus Mutasa (party's secretary for administration). He was not happy with the way the economy was being handled then, especially corruption in the government. Minister Sylvester Nguni, the late general Solomon Mujuru, professor Jonathan Moyo (the psycho wish-washy professor, whom I still blame for most of the problems Zimbabwe is now dealing with, especially the distortion of the news media ministry). Back then, he was running the government, on a de-facto basis, as the information minister, at around year 2000. All these individuals were said to have visited the ambassadors of the USA, and had leaked information on ZANU-PF, and would call the ambassador, especially Dell, the often referred to as ambassador Hell by Mugabe; to remove Mugabe from power.

ZANU-PF is now a tense party as I write this diary. It seems there is a huge fall-out between its senior members, along those faction lines; Mujuru versus Mnangagwa camps. Most of Mnangagwa's people were not involved in this, so they are pushing for the disciplining of the Mujuru's camp, the bulk of which were seeing the ambassadors. For Mnangagwa's camp, it's an opportunity to silence Mujuru's camp, or to destroy it, altogether. The state security is said to have started the investigations, so have the attorney general Tomana, who I must admit has been quiet all along after being silenced, and made to look stupid by the MDC who didn't want him to keep his post in the GNU government, but barely kept it through support from Mugabe. Now it seems he has found a new lease of life.

I was discussing with friends about this, and my feeling is nothing drastic is going to come out of these investigations or meetings (the politburo tomorrow is meeting about this). There are a lot of big people involved, so pushing them out will only weaken ZANU-PF as we head to the election, which is untenable. It will intensify the factional wars between the two camps as well, all the more. Mugabe is now isolated, it seems. I would like to hear what he will say, or do. Is he going to clean up the presidium? Such double standards from ZANU-PF are unprecedented, and all the more exciting.

*****

I returned back to the editor my first edit returns of the novel, KEYS IN THE RIVER. I feel so fantastic...the stories in the book are fantastic, fabulous. They now have an American feel, maybe it comes from working with an American editor. She is great, not fussing, and very open minded. I am enjoying working with her.

*****

We are imploding; our relationship is imploding with Miss K. I feel I have come to a point where I might never be able to return back. I am getting prepared, everyday, to keep going. I haven't seen her for over a week, haven't talked to her for a long time now. There is no push in me to reach out and come to some understanding with her. I think, I feel I have been fighting a self-defeating war with her, and that it is now time to let it go. Its hell, I feel like someone very important for my own existence has left me somewhere out there, and I don't know where to go, the way back to myself. This is how I am feeling, but I have no other way, than to figure out my way back to me, maybe to balance.

Friday, September 16, 2011

Some stupid thief came our place once more, with the intent to break in, but couldn't find a way in. he had to steal the head of our bathroom shower tape. It costs 4 dollars on the open market, and I am now 4 dollars set behind, but that's okay. I wonder, if he was going to be caught, or be beaten up, for only 4 dollars! It's pathetic to have such a kind of life; hopeless.

*****

I am crashing out of the relationship with her. The biggest part of me is urging me to keep going, wherever. Yeah, there are difficult feelings I have to get a good hang over, but it's always a part of the deal...

13

Age Has No Numbers?

I have always thought and I still feel that it's difficult to write love stories. They are some love stories that I feel, even if I were to manage to write something down about them whatever I could have written couldn't have expressed much about those stories. Only through bleeding, only through burning into ash and only through my death could these stories be expressed. All that I could do was to try to say my story without going through to these extremities and this is one of those love stories.

Sometime in April, 2004, we were organising for a fundraising activity, St. Vincent fundraising at my local parish St. Agnes Catholic Church. This was a youth outreach program to the community, and we were raising money to feed the poor of our parish. I was the Vice-Chairman of the fundraising committee for this function and in the same committee was this sweet, sweet girl. The first day I saw her, we were having our first meeting, outside the church, in the sun, on the church lawns. I said "hello" to her. She said "hello" to me back, smiling sweetly. With a shaft of sheer male appreciation, I took in her tumble of black hair curls, laughing brown eyes, and mile long legs encased in black tights beneath a short cherry-red skirt. This enticing combination made me almost mad. Oh, Sharon (that's not her actual name) was so sweet. Aren't they all sweet in the beginning! Yes, this child woman was so full of sparrows, but it was her sweetness and her tall curvy figure that crucified me straight away.

I didn't know Sharon for she was coming from another youth group St. Agnes and Alois youth group. I was from St. Simon Peter and Maria youth group. It was not a given that I would know every other youth at this church unless of course there were in the same group with me. So, when I came to know about Sharon, it was when we made this same committee. We also came to talk and sometimes just acted polite and sweet to each other. Isn't that how trouble always starts? It was Sharon's child-like laughter and beautiful smile that I became instantly aware of and everything got to revolve around her. Down side of this I hated it. I really do hate it for I want to have a little bit of power. Strangely, it is power play that's more interesting in a relationship. You wonder what a relationship is, I know. But that's what I would have preferred.

It's like I would be a disciple of some sort to these love-mad activities pining for redemption and for heaven from the outside because I know that from the inside, it was too good for me. I am sorry I prefer to be a tourist here, holding the object of love from the outside than being a pilgrim because I know being a pilgrim could only result in me getting hurt. But, when you have to spent a lot of time together with this object of your love, this uninvolved posture melts away easily because she becomes more human, more like the girl next door, so that you would get to have a little bit of confidence to look directly at this image of all the things that you have always wanted your ideal woman to have. This lack of space doesn't bother you anymore; you don't become annoyed, or fall into silence as you used to do with other girls.

You don't only pray to this girl. You also believe in her, especially when you were with her. Maybe when she is smiling sweetly at you, or her eyes are focused on you, she is attentive to you. She blushes, when you lock eyes with her. You feel like you could just hold her in your arms and absorb her into your being so that she would always be there in you whenever you breathe, smile, laugh, sleep, eat or do everything else. When you are with her, you also lose your sense of large, ambiguous things. I think a lot of it is just pure infatuation, and whoever said infatuation is not love?

Sharon would avoid all the other guys at this church who were some hissing bees after her nectar. She would come over to me and hang out with me even before I had plucked enough courage to tell her that I was some crazy-lots about her. You should know how this made me feel like.

For a couple of weeks or a month or so after I had told Sharon about my feelings, I hit the roof. Loving her to distraction, I was in irretrievable land. It felt good to be me, to have this, and to see how it was coming together. It took the two of us to push the relationship into place. This feeling filled me with confidence. Little did I know that this dream could easily be conflated by the process of making ordinary human interchanges and conflicts and that we would grow more and more apart and estranged?

I had so much to tell her when I knew I would be meeting her. When we got together, though, I said very little. Most of the times, we were just silent, not a probing silence but just good silence, but still kept company of the other. I should have tried harder to be more verbal. I suppose it could have helped me unlock her. Talking in a relationship is good because you can get to tell her about how you feel in other words other than the "I love you" phraseology every time. Maybe, if I had talked to her more about myself, then I could really have encouraged her to talk a little bit more about herself too. But, I had no words for the way I felt. I still do not have words for that.

I also wanted her to feel that I am not going to break everything up, that it would be safe for her to pick up a crate of eggs or a glass of wine. So, all that I did was to say, *I love you, I love you, I love you.* That's the best I could express how I felt. I literally experienced withdrawal when I was away from Sharon. I was dead inside until I got another fix of her again. It was a prayer situation, the situation I was in; believing that she instinctually knows the things that I couldn't tell her. Just as a prayer doesn't say all that we want our God to know, yet he knows all that we really want, all that we are asking of him. In most cases, we don't even know what to tell God, the right words but he knows. After all, she was my god!

Sharon was nineteen, so beautiful and fragile. So unpredictable! They are like that at this age, aren't they? Yes, they still want to be teenagers, but confuse the world with their maturity. The thing is that they are just girls trying to be women, what they know of a woman. I am so sorry for this sarcasm, but this is the truth: there are too hot to handle at this age. I was thirty then. The number thirty; has its own magical contents and complexities, but that depends on the person. But nineteen, like a villanelle consisting of nineteen lines, five tarcets and one concluding quatrain, is nineteen. Enough of this, juxtaposing people with age for age has no numbers, they say and I agree. Even though now I am in my middle thirties, I still feel so young at heart. I agree, like I have said, that age has no numbers, but it wasn't like that with her.

I knew Sharon was interested in knowing how old I was, but for some time she had no courage to ask me about that. She even asked her best friend, Lorraine, to ask me about my age on her behalf, but I told Lorraine,

"No, no, friend, we don't do it that way."

If Sharon was interested in knowing my age, then she had to ask herself. Lorraine understood. Eventually, Sharon plucked enough courage to ask me. I told her I was thirty that year. Instantly everything changed, or seemed to have changed. She started to bicker badly about our ages and age differences.

"You are too old to be my father, John." She would say, over and over again. This nettled me.

"How could she dare compare me with her father when she was just about ten years younger than me?" But, like some bloody shrew, Sharon began to use this as a sticking point in whatever disagreements we had. She would say, cruelly,

"You will die and leave me a widow." She also began to tear into my flesh and each time the healing would take a bit longer. Her blows were going deeper and deeper into my soul. I fought her like hell, too. Sometimes I would ask her,

"How do you know you won't die before me, Sharon?" Like I said I don't believe in numbers and here she was trying to define all that I felt for her by quantifying it into numbers. Of course I couldn't have had it that way, so I fought her.

The more we fought over this, the more the aura of our magical land became the grotesque limbo land of Edward Burra's paintings. Our barbed-wire voices tangled at every space. Even when there was really nothing to say to each other, we always found something to say just to hurt the other. The weight of this knowledge, pushing a cracked spine, so by the time she left for university studies in Gweru in September of that same year, I was just holding onto one string that she would eventually come around some day and accept me for who I was, not for my age. The truth is that and, I would like to set it out now, Sharon never told me; in all the years we were seeing each other that she loved me. It's not a huge thing that she didn't, for not a lot of girls can say that to a guy, especially shy young girls. A boy sometimes just looks for signs. If a girl is willing to spend a lot of time with you, then that's already a beginning. Even though I could see glimpses of things in her eyes, Sharon couldn't quite bring herself to shoot me with her eye's soft voice of love, no. Yet, I badly wanted to hear those words, at least just once. A man sometimes wants to hear those words!

Sharon left for Gweru, 300kms away from Chitungwiza. On her part, I think, she started drifting apart, but I couldn't have entertained that thought because she had once promised me that one day she would tell me about her feelings for me. My job was to continue cultivating this patch of land and take good care of it, so that someday in the future, I could have good harvests out of it. I didn't give up so I kept phoning her, sometimes more than once a day, sometimes I would text her some sweet and cool messages. When she came back for the holidays, I was there for her. Time activated and flew away on this hoping-for-the-best out of the relationship.

Two years down the line, she returned back to stay in Chitungwiza and later in Harare and she was now doing her year of industrial attachments at a firm in Harare. Even though I still was pushing for my cause, I discovered that things had taken another swerve with her, that we had made the curve as if it wasn't there and trundled along the silence of that road. Like a long-sought-after-road-to-the-heavens, there was still a window, a brief window here and there and a love already anticipating its own absence. Beneath all that, we were still trying to make things work out by building some shrine of some sort to everything that was already lacking by measuring our love against time lost being together. As long as it was one or two degrees closer to what could be endured, it sufficed enough for us to be there for a little while for the other. But, like a beautiful coil, our love continued to rise to the heavens as a never-ending dream until what had gone out into the skies was all of our love and soon was forgotten, leaving a cell-block cage crammed with our long tossed-away time.

When we are in such life or love-embodied affairs, it's not easy to come to terms with that and we take a lot of time making excuses as to why things have turned out this bad with our adored subjects. I think it is us trying to go through this unpleasant circumstance without hurting too much. By the end of that third year and by the end of that year of her industrial attachment, deep down my heart, I knew that there was now very little between us, that somehow I had lost Sharon over the years. I can't still say when I lost her. I think it would be impossible to say when for it is a matter of the heart. Can anyone tell his heart that it shouldn't be feeling the things it is still feeling when it is feeling the things it is feeling. There is neither top nor bottom of the world, neither an end to eastwards or to the westwards, only the way your heart accepts as best. One has to wait until the inner system has dealt with failure of a relationship to have real closure. I wish I can be more rational about it and do some mathematical combinations and permutations to solve this complex number problem just to confirm that her departure really was because of the numbers only. The truth is that and I was so stupid not to think about it, she was still growing up and growing up has its own pressures, its own permutations and combinations. Nineteen is the time when you start panning out and nobody controls the outcome, not even love. It's an out-of-life experience that you would be going through when you are nineteen. One can only hope that when they come out of the growth, they would still want to be with us. Deep down, that's what I pinned for.

She came out differently. She didn't want to be with me anymore. I still wanted her. The truth is that you can't force yourself into that mixture. I am so sorry that I couldn't just kill myself so that I could get out of this land. I am stuck in this land like a pig stuck in its own faecal. I can only hum along to David Archuleta's "All I want is you" as I write this story.

Yes, the years may have passed by. Yes, she is still be catching my eye. Yes, she is still improving... with age like old wine, they say. *Yes, I love who she is now.* What is that? The truth is that she doesn't want you, yet you want her. It's nice to say those words on a piece of paper, but try to write them in your heart. Will them into your heart, then you will get to know it's another thing altogether.

It doesn't happen for you!

What still beats the hell out of me is despite my love for her, I lost her. Sharon is human, I know that. Doubt is the scourge of our everyday life and she is not an exception. Yes, she could have doubted how I felt for her some other times. It is like that, shit happens! But, she came to a conclusion that what I felt for her was not good enough. This thought still boggles me. She must have known that she had me at her fingertips and only a thumb of her fingers could have brought me to her, in whatever mode she wanted me to be. But I didn't know who she wanted me to be and nobody could tell me. I could have sung her favourite songs for her, become Justin Timberlake or P-square. If she wanted me to be Brad Pitt, I could have become Brad for her. If she wanted, then she and I could even have adopted a United Nations family of her whims, whines, feelings or even misbegotten ideas. But the truth is that she just didn't want to be with me.

Maybe, it could be this in-your-face attitude that I took with her by pestering her about us through phoning her, through creating situations in which we had to meet that kept us on the drift, all the more and the thin air of her heart kept gobbling us and punting me out. Maybe, I should have left the relationship when there were many hints lingering around her: university studies, age differences, avoidance, and rejection. When my mind told me to take a hike, I did not because my heart wasn't ready for departure.

This was how the road was like to me. I loved, cried, laughed, believed, and got hurt. Pain and happiness intertwined and became the normal way of my life for five years. I could only kill her or she could only kill me and killing me was the only thing that I could do. It was the only thing that I had courage for.

Four years later, I left Zimbabwe for South Africa. Perhaps I had the dream of escaping the complexities of this relationship as the intervals between one's goings and comings sever the years as a hyphen severs the flow of a sentence. Yet, a couple of months after my departure, I was phoning Sharon already. She started being nice to me on the phone and asked for some money, a couple of times. She was such a sucker to think that she could scrounge money from me that easily because I loved her. I promised her that I would be sending her some, but I never did and never will. The reason is, to begin with, I didn't have the money to send to her. Even if I had some, I knew I would never have done that. Sharon had lately been treating me as a second hand boyfriend, before I left for South Africa. She had never really wanted me in her life, and why the bloody hell did she think I could just sent her money on such a silver plate? For goodness sake, I am not a bank. Had she shown or told me that she was wrong about how she treated me all those years? That, she now wanted things to work out between us and, if she had given me a little bit to grab and hold onto, maybe I'd buy into it and could have given her the money she was asking for.

I could have borrowed money from somebody to send it over to her if I wanted to. You may think that I am stingy. Sure, money is not such a big deal. Money should be shared with loved ones. It is just a bunch of numbers. One thousand dollars is one thousand numbers of dollars, so was my age to her. Remember that! I don't care that much about the money. All I care is that I have just enough of it to get me by. I will throw every penny in if I can help ones I deeply care for any day. This time, it's about my feelings. I don't have any intention to let my feelings get played by anyone. I will do some serious emotional budgeting. It's just so unfortunate that she still couldn't figure out how much I really loved her after all these years of my devotion towards her!

As we started talking again, she encouraged me to return for the Christmas holiday. Although I thought it was still too early to return back, I was sort of enticed by the suggestion. Contemplating with the suggestion, I asked her one day if she would see me when I go back home. She categorically said no! Afterwards, I stopped phoning her and drifted for another six months. When I phoned her again, she was angry with me because I hadn't been phoning her.

This has always been difficult for me to process; why Sharon would complain if I stopped phoning her and that when I kept in touch with her, all she could do was to make it such a painful experience for me by bickering and fighting me all the time. Maybe, it was her habit towards people; she once said that she was difficult to deal with? I would always feel like I am in an emotional rollercoaster when I am with her. It's like you love someone deeply, but she says she doesn't love you and wants you to go. Of course, when you try to go, she would complain that you shouldn't have tried to go. The next day, when you phone her again, she would tell you that she really like you to go and leave her alone.

Since the last talk on the phone with Sharon, it has been hell for me. I made my best effort not to call her. Every day, I fight this urge to log her numbers onto my cell phone and press the dial button. Anyone who has gone through a drug experience would understand what I am talking about here and how difficult it is to get over the temptation. There are times when I tried to close off my mind and stop thinking of her, hoping that pain will be minimised.

At least, I am far removed from her. There is no possibility that we might meet in the streets. All that I can do is to fight this urge to phone her. I am not saying that it's easy or I am succeeding, no. I am not even saying it is helping that much either for healing this wound because she is all that I still think of, if I think of anyone at all. She is all that I have thought of all these years even when I lied to myself that I was over her. I am now in love with this other girl whom I would be dating, but a couple of days, weeks, or even some months later, I might start calling Sharon again.

This is what I have been dealing with. I am now tired of lying to myself and to these girls. For this past year or so I haven't looked at any other woman because I didn't want to waste their time. I am going to remain faithful alone for as long as it takes. I want to prove to Sharon that moving on is possible, if I stay faithful to the idea. But, it is still only when I am thinking of her that I feel complete. It's only when I am thinking of her when I feel my heart in my chest. It's only when I am thinking of her, frozen in time squares, that I feel complete. I still want all these feelings boxed up by their own magic without my having to touch any of it or the things in it. This is the hardest part: to let her go.

I will try to stay away from her if that's what I have to do for the rest of my life. I won't try to call her. I will try everyday not to even think of her if that's what I have to do so as not to complicate my situation all over again. Maybe, I will be successful. Maybe, I have been mentally preparing my mind for this. I am not promising myself that I would always be successful. It is my mind and heart that I don't know what to do with. I can deal with my mind during the day. It's my heart I don't have a clue on.

My heart is a different genre altogether. It is a trip hammer thumping every second and its beat is louder and louder, twenty four hours a day, seven days a week, fifty two weeks a year, year after year. Every muscle in my heart, every iota in my heart, every vein in my heart, and every ounce of blood in my heart chime a song, *Sharon*. Perhaps, we just weren't meant to get out of this! So, who is going to monkey-wrench us out of this ruin?

14

Gathering Evidence
Diaries (2013-2014)

Wednesday 1 January 2013

I have never had such a terribly painful and boring Christmas period as the last one I have just had. I spent most of my time dealing with stress, illness (cholesterol) and general angst. Last year was a good year for me but for those last few days. But I am through it all. I am feeling better now

*****

It was raining since 6 in the morning. It's almost midday now. It has stopped raining. The temperatures are a beautiful cloudy. I like it! I like it! I like it!

*****

Yesterday I started the 10 days of fasting. There are 10 days of fasting and prayer directed by our parish priest, father Joseph Matare, in which we will be meeting at the church for the prayers, talks and Mass. I have shied away from participating in these 10 days before, for the last 2 years since they were introduced but this year I am in. I feel I want to develop a closer relationship with myself, with God. I have doubted whether my relationship with God is still good, for years now, so I would like to push it to become closer. I still talk or pray regularly to God but I feel stunted or as if I am in a comfort zone with him. I need to feel him more, better, closer. There is more I want, would like to achieve on. It's about me, too. Sometimes I feel I have lost my way; that I am getting more lost with every day; that I don't feel closer to myself as I used to do. There is mostly too much psychic (not too dark, though…, just that kind that's restless and frustrating) traffic, sometimes I have really bad vibes with myself and it's all these I am trying to deal with. It was all these things I was trying to think about during the Christmas time and I wasn't getting headway.

I felt so lonely as if I had travelled too far and I have forgotten my way back, home (in the sense of a place that makes you grounded and happy). I have also been writing or thinking on this idea that I am now hitting at 40 this year, and that I should be making my way, or on the way to finding my way home. A couple of days or so ago I watched Toni Morrison (American writer) being interviewed about her latest novel, HOME, on F24, by Em Jackson, saying the home could be , *there is no home at all.* It's like negating a negative to find a positive. Morrison felt there was no home, and if there was no home, she was trying, in her novel, to construct such a home for herself. It's like the concept of trying to build something from negating everything until you get to where it all started. I am thinking, I have been thinking I am now on the way to finding my own home. I have thought about this and I have been writing about it, too. I don't want it to be philosophical or ideological or even a literary take of it. I want to really experience it. Sometimes I feel there a bigger part of me I have frozen over the years and haven't explored that much and in this journey I would like to unfold, unfreeze these parts. I have to really know this part of me and these 10 days of fasting might also afford me an opportunity to figure out what parts of my life I need to unfreeze, to explore. One that easily comes to my mind and might be the most important thing is on relationships. It's no longer about me and a girl relationship. It's pretty much about all facets of relationships. I feel I have been lagging, sometimes quiet terribly. I don't have close relationships with my friends anymore, and I am not making much effort anymore, rather it is them who are trying harder to stay closer to me. With my family it is improving but it needs more working on. With a girl it is disappointing. I really need this to start working. I have tried a lot of girls around, this last year without much. It's still there is no relationship worth talking of; they are always flirting out of my life like mayflies. I feel like I am running circles around the beginnings of relationships and then that's that, no growing of these relationships to really enjoy them. I want to do the journeying with a girl, enjoying the ups and downs of it all and get to something. I want to be walking. I need more, but the journey is static.

*****

I want to make the journey. I am going to make the journey. I want to settle down someday soon, and this year, if possible. I want to continue with the journey in different aspects of my life. I want to discover me, to find my home. Now, it's the journey to find my way, to discover what my home is, with whom, I don't know.

*****

In the fasting, I am doing a gradual fasting, or immersion into it. Today I am fasting up to at least mid-day. Then I want to push it further tomorrow until I can fast for longer periods.

I have always had issues about fasting, some of which I explored indirectly in the essay, THE HUNGER STRIKE in the collection of non-fictions and essays, *Zimbabwe: The Blame Game*, 2013. We are working with the editor and publisher Roselyne Jua to have this book published, and the process is taking more of my time. It's a journey I am going to make this year too, having the book published!

*****

I want us to work things out with Colleen (it's a pseudonym I am going to use). I have to find some way to work things with her. At least try to push or pull for a relationship and see how things will pan out. Despite some couple of things I don't like about her, I think she is a good girl. I can feel the potential in her. It's another of the journeys I will be making this year

*****

13.00 pm
I am so hungry!

*****

I am about to turn in now for the night. It's roughly past 9 at night. I attended Mass and the fasting programme at the church. It was one of the best Mass and prayer I have had in years. I talked and talked to God about the issues I have highlighted in this diary. I felt very close to him. I am about to turn in. what's left are night prayers

Oh! Before I close for the day, today I was sogged down to the bone with rain, a deluge when coming back home from the church. It rained hard from about 5 pm up to now (9pm), it's still raining. I am unfazed by all that. If it rains badly tomorrow again, the same time, it is going to rain me down as I return from church, again. If this is going to be happening to me for the rest of the fasting time, bring it on! I even feel cleansed by all these rains…and very happy.

*****

Let me pray.

Thursday 3 January 2013

I am happy with myself, I think quiet happy. When I am happy with myself I write a lot. I have just written a travel article, *My Volmoed Journey*, on my journey to South Africa for the Caine workshop, in March 2012. For the whole of last year I couldn't get it going, but for the last few hours ago I have written and completed it. Friends next door, Catherine and Carol are back from holidaying with their Uncles and Aunts in South Africa. I have talked to them. I missed them. It's nice to see them.

*****

Last night I had a fun dream. I had travelled to some place. I don't even remember, why. When I arrived at the place, which I thought, at that first moment of dreaming, as a local place I know, I discovered it was frozen in ice. It was a dam frozen, and another part was a lake, which at first wasn't frozen. I thought of crossing it, I don't know if it was because of fear but I told myself I could take the long way and cross it off at the top end where it ends. I had to be on the other side of it, so I obsessed about it and loitered around the frozen dam. Later the lake was frozen, too. The place resembled Volmoed in South Africa, the environment of it but it felt like it was somewhere else. At one time I am trying to finish off some writing. I am at the workshop where I have to produce a story. I am very confident I am going to produce a really good story. I obsess a lot on top of this ice. I get paid some money for the story. It was in pounds sterling. I am happy. Eventually I tell myself I have to take the path across this lake, even though I have already crossed it several times in my obsessiveness whilst it was iced. I take the journey and then I wake up.

*****

I am continuing with my fasting. The idea is I have to eat little and start eating after 12 pm every day. Of course I am hungry, but I am okay. I am happy. Does fasting make one happy? I will read the bible, I love reading the book of Romans, and I will pray in the afternoons before eating. Later I will attend prayers and Mass at the church, St. Agnes Catholic Church, Zengeza, Chitungwiza, which is in Zengeza 3

Saturday 5 January 2013
It's raining and raining, damp, very nice. It rained throughout the night. It is about to rain. I miss her. I last saw her last Sunday. I like her a lot. I tell myself I want this. Isn't

most of it about telling yourself you need someone, want to be with someone, only that one person.

*****

I am continuing with my fasting and prayers and it's the 5th day. A couple of days ago there was talk of Christianity and the family. The priest, father Matare, talked of love between family members that got me arrested and interested. He said parents should not choose or show favouritism toward children, and that they should treat children equally. Then someone asked how can a parent balance out love, and what if it's the child that is feeling she is being side-lined when in actual fact the parent doesn't think or feel they were doing that. Father Matare said the fact that a kid feels that way should be of cause of concern to the parent. A parent should try to make or work toward making the kid not to feel that way. It should not be about how the parent feels about things but what the kid feels the parent is doing. It's a tough call but very much interesting. He even pointed out the kind of sick, destructive rivalry that will result from all that if it's not sorted out by referring to the story of Joseph in the bible, who was sold out by his brothers to the Egyptians because of this sibling rivalry created through favouritism. It's a difficult thing to practice and contemplate on. God in the bible showed favouritism to Isaac, and to many others. I don't think it's possible to love two different people, equally. Is it possible? Favouritism will show out no matter how much you might not try to show it.

Another very interesting aspect he also touched on is there is as much each family can try to pray for unity, love or togetherness. He said sometimes we just have to accept that it is not working and that our families are meant to be that disfigured or hellholes, and try to live with that. He said we have to accept that crucifix and carry it every day. It's another tough call, but I think I understand that.

*****

Generally I am great with myself, feel very close to myself and my creator.

Friday 11 January 2013

The fasting is over. It ended yesterday. It was hugely successful for me for I am very happy with myself. I feel more connected to myself, connected to God. I feel settled into myself. I know I am going to face this year well. I have dealt with all the fears and toxic doubts I had about myself and others. I believe I love Colleen but I am also ready to let her go if she wants me to go. That's now what I am working on with her. I want to know if she wants me to go. Then I will go. It's a sad fact of life and I would if it were to be done in another way. I have learned, if you love someone you should be willing to let them go when they want to go.

*****

It's slightly windy, and humid. It rained yesterday last night, so it isn't that hot, but humid. I feel a bit restless. I have talked to her a bit. At least it seems she is now listening to me or trying to hear what I am saying, even though she doesn't always get it right. It's good to know she is trying to understand or just listening and talking to me. All that I want is for us to always be able to talk to each other despite what will become of us now. Talk is always good.

My heart is bursting with love for her; I feel like an unused, disused pit hole, no one wants to pile their shit in it. I want to tell her these words, "I love you, I love you, I love you…", until she understands the hell of it!

Thursday 17 January 2013

This state I am in, this place, this situation I am in possesses me like a monster demon. I have struggled to get free from it without success. It is because I am afraid of the outside environments of this situation, this life. How could I be afraid when I want to go there, to get to that outside? I am single, lonely single. I don't seem to hold a girl down to relationship worth talking about. I am always trying, and be more willing to try more. It's frustrating, defeating to realise she didn't stick a bit longer on me, to me, in me. I am running against myself- a lot of the times, to make it out with these girls. I feel I am corroding my inner true self-worth to hold these down, and even that don't seem enough. I am tired of my condition. Is it a shadow I can't seem to walk away from…yet I want to walk into someone and stay inside that someone.

Tuesdays 22 January 2013

Yesterday something extraordinary (maybe unusual is the right word here) happened in Chitungwiza. I hope it would change people's lives here permanently, profoundly maybe. It was somewhere after mid-afternoon, the sky was with very few fluffy clouds. I was restless, so I was reading a bit trying to hold down that restlessness; sometimes I tried to think or to write something without success and some other times slept, dozed

141

off for most of the day, and then all of a sudden, *boom*…, like a bomb or something like that. It wasn't like an earthquake shake or tremours. I remembered when somewhere Kariba dam had a tremor and we felt it all the way in my rural home in Nyanga, over 500 km from Kariba, so I knew the tremours of the earth's sneezes. It wasn't, it was more like lightening, more like a bomb, and it was surprising to hear that sound in the clear skies, worse to think of it as a bomb sound in Chitungwiza. I woke up from my dozing position, got outside, and checked around the street, everyone was doing the same. There was nothing in the street. It had happened further than our street. People started speculating, some rushed-off to the source.

I returned back to my dozing meditation position and environment, still I had no inspiration for anything. I didn't sleep or meditated longer as the stories started piercing my worlds, unravelling what had happened. Some saying it was a bomb, some saying it was a gas stove, some saying a lot of people had died. Yes, it had happened in Zengeza 2, at number 4 Ndororo Street, just a house off the corner of Ndororo Street and Mukomberanwa drive, on the way to Zengeza 3. Those who witnessed it said there were a strong wind and an explosion that shook this household and others surrounding it, breaking down and cracking houses around this place, 4 men and a small kid died. These four included a business man (taxi operator) who owned the *Barcelona* fleet of taxis, whom it seems, had come to consult a N'anga (tradition faith healer), whom some said had also come from somewhere, a week before. It is said whilst this N'anga was doing his treatment ceremony on this businessman that's when a lightning struck the place. The general accepted version in the gossip torn streets is that a lightning struck this place, and that it is seeded lightening, by this N'anga or someone else, maybe someone the businessman and N'anga wanted to hurt. In our culture or tradition there is a belief that some N'angas can manufacture (or engineer) a lightning strike, even in clear skies like yesterday's skies and can use this to struck off enemies, and so this is the version that was propagating rapidly. Even in the news at 8, the national broadcaster, *Zimbabwe Television* reported the incident much the same way.

The speculation is now it's either this businessman wanted to hurt someone, or he wanted to disposes himself of some Tokoloshis (half human, half monster beings) used to help accrue wealth with, that had helped him accumulate the wealth he had (the taxi fleet), and that the N'anga wasn't strong enough and was overpowered by these Tokoloshis. It's a massive gossip and speculating realm now opened up in Chitungwiza, and the entire country. The people I stay with (who lodges some rooms at our place), when it happened they were travelling back to the city from their rural homes after an extended end of year holiday there, but when they arrived home they already knew a lot about it, even more than I knew who was in the area when it happened. They say some relative, in Rusape town, 200kms from here had called them, telling them of this spectacle. It is how gossip flies off the shelves in Zimbabwe, like scarce commodities.

I know this Sunday, in the churches around Chitungwiza and Zimbabwe; the bible thumpers are going to have a great go at this story. Either way you look at it, it shows massive promise to make it into the churches; comparing God's power over us mortals will be the point of entry of every sermon. I don't want to be preachy but I feel, I would like to think it would put a lot of things into perspective. Those who are still looking for wealth through these shoddy means are going to think twice before consulting a N'anga again. Those who think they are very powerful spiritually, like the motley lot of these N'angas and the prophetic faith healers that are ubiquitous all over the country are going to be very careful. Or they are going to be more daring. There is a challenge in this episode. Chitungwiza is now a battleground between different opposing spiritual worlds. There are a lot of bible thumpers and prophetic man of God doing crazy miracles, even the inappropriately popular prophet Makandiwa has located his church from Harare to Chitungwiza, and is on the forefront of this miracle making madness.

A few months ago he was said to have made bald headed people have their hair back in their heads. Another prophet, Hubert Angels was said to be putting money into his congregant's pockets, miraculously. And who wouldn't want to go a church where instead of the church man taking your hard earned toil, rather you are given what you never earned. It's like manna from heaven. I think most of the miracles are crazy miracles, stupid hoodwinking jobs to attract more attention and more rent from the desperate people of Chitungwiza. My exuberant priest, father Lovemore Gutu, in last Sunday's homily said if someone can be able to put money into your pocket or account or cell phone account, he can also be able to take money from you, thus he was attacking Angels. These supposed prophets are super rich and still counting. It might boil down to Chitungwiza is the poorest of all Zimbabwean cities. It is a ghetto hell hole of very poor people, but all the same, ambitious. This is like a cooking pot for creating the drive or ambition to succeed and vault one's self off this city. Thus Chitungwiza is a hotbed of talents in different fields in the country. You can say without being wrong that Chitungwiza gave Zimbabwe half of talents in the following among other fields, Music, all art fields, all sports, media talents, technical talents. If you raise from this dunk city and become successful it is a classic case of from rugs to riches, and since there are not many opportunities in the city itself, people are now resorting to getting wealth through shoddy means, exemplified by the 4 Ndororo street episode, the Makandiwas et el. It's a battleground for evil and good- it seems a lot now think it's the only way to get head over their poverty, through evil. I am sorry I was a bit preachy, but it is an interesting, very interesting place to live in, as well. I will unravel this story as it grips us here.

*****

It's humid hot, a summer day and everything is going on the usual way here. I am fine, still hung up with personal stuff. There is someone who is attracting my attention, whom I knew a couple of years ago, and I had given up on her, the Miss K in IT'S NOT ABOUT ME dairies. I am sure I DON'T want this in my life again. It was one of those things that possessed me yesterday and also I had seen Colleen at the church on Sunday. It was the quietest feeling I have had over a girl that I had with her on Sunday. She came to greet me and I was polite with her. But yesterday I thought of her (stubbornly, my mind doesn't seem to stop). I am conflicted. It's a complex situation. I still have feelings for her, and its hurting me bad. I think she is hurting, as well. But I don't know, whatever!

*****

Yesterday on the news there was a tentative announcement from Kgalema Motlanthe (South African president) who is the

145

mediator in the talks between the MDC and ZANU-PF that there has been common ground between the two parties on the constitution making endeavour. That very soon it would be presented to the parliament and the people for voting and a referendum. It's interesting to hear this. I am not sure what common ground has been found, since the two parties had divergent views on a lot of issues they couldn't agree on in the draft. Has ZANU-PF bite the humble pie and allowed for the power diluting draft they were so set against all through the whole of last year, or has the MDC sold out on the people's wishes and expectations for power mongering reasons. I need to know what the compromises are. Zimbabwe feels, everyday, like a lost cause. I don't know, I have not much faith we will ever reach Nirvana land with these political players we have. We have already given up on a lot of things that we fought for the last 10 years or so and we can only lose so much more with this constitution until a time when it's not worth it. We seem to be heading towards that point.

Wednesday 23 January 2013

The plot thickens and the stories are abounded and deepen. I am no longer happy in writing this diary anymore, because it has become personal. I know the owners of 4 Ndororo Street. I have been friends; we are distant relatives with them. I have known the daughter of this place for years, somewhere in the late 1990s, she rented (with her cousin brother family) some rooms next door, and that's when we got to know each other. With my sisters they are still very close. We call her sister Via (for Violet) and it was disturbing to hear it had happened at their place. At first, just the term 4 Ndororo street had tagged something in my mind, but I couldn't figure out what it was, until my sister, Judith, came through my place last night and reminded me it was sister Via's family home, and then everything became clear to me. I knew why, all along, something was wrong and I had wrongfully assigned it to relationships. It was this that was obsessing me. I get to feel like that when something bad is going to happen. A street friend, Prosper Mlambo came through an hour after it had happened. He wanted to pick me up so as to accompany him to the place to see what was really happening and I had said, no. I told him it might be the place of someone I know or I might see someone I know maimed or dead and I didn't want that. Delayed knowledge of a disaster somehow seem to prepare you to better face it, as long as you generally know something has happened and you don't know who has been affected, yet. It is the time to get to terms with any eventuality, such that when you know that there is someone you know who has been a victim of it, then you have already prepared to face it. I knew then, something was wrong, and that's why I refused to go. Only to now realise last night that I knew all along. It is the place of someone I know. Fortunately none of the dead or maimed is part of this family. What follows is hurtful for me to write. I need time to process this discovery. I still feel restless, like I am living outside my skin.

Thursday 24 January 2013

I am assaulted by theories, plots, gossips… Chitungwiza is abounding with it, sizzling with talk of it. People are talking madly around this issue. I think we have moved from the initial shock part and people are trying to figure out what really happened at number 4 Ndororo Street. I will keep using this title of 4 Ndororo Street to remove myself from personal connections of it, and it is now a mythical, enigmatic name, even though it's just a place I have known. Here is another story. Sometime beginning of this month, on the 6th January, their long time tenant for 12 years disappeared without giving notice of leave, or a forwarding address, so the rooms became vacant. This departing lodger owed my relatives over $1 000 in United States terms, and that's a fortune in Zimbabwe, so they decided to disappear. These relatives decided to replace the disappeared tenant with others. They were two well-groomed guys, suited to the hilt, who came looking for a place for their brother. The owners of 4 Ndororo Street asked them where that brother was, and they said he was bogged down with other stuff, and was coming from another town, far away and that's why they took the duty of helping him secure lodgings. Not knowing they were creating problems for themselves, these relatives of mine took these people's money and gave them the place to stay. On 10th January the tenant came with his family. Nobody had told my relatives this tenant was a N'anga, only to discover it as he had settled in, as people started coming from all over the country looking for this N'anga, being helped with their problems. The father of my relatives was staying in the rural areas and when he heard of this he came to Chitungwiza from Nyanga where he stays to give notice of evacuation by month end to this new tenant. The day he left for home is the day the property, 4 Ndororo street went up in flames, taking with it 5 lives, including an innocent 1 month old tot, a kid of one of the lodgers, an innocent tenant. Here are the ghoulish details.

The woman, the businessman's wife and the other tenants said there was this huge white wind that shook up things and the N'anga was stirring his medicine clay pot. In that wind, they said they saw a black thing with white lips, the purported Tokoloshi the businessman wanted to part with in this ceremony. The woman run out as the place was struck by a bolt, some say of lightening, and some say even the N'anga was hit off when he tried to run out. The 5 were cut into pieces. The businessman's scalp was found hung on top of the roofs; pieces of flesh were sprayed all over the property. When the fire brigade came they had to concentrate on picking up of the pieces, jumping over licking blood, splattered all over the place.

Those who survived included the wife of the N'anga, the businessman's wife and the mother of the kid and they denied there was a Tokoloshi dumping ceremony, even the relatives of the N'anga are saying he is not a N'anga as such but a faith healer of the apostolic sect known as Johann Nguwo Tsvuku (Johann of red cloth). Yet this sect is known of practicing both traditional and Christian rituals, and they believe in an eye for an eye. This sect came out of the original, larger apostolic sect, Johann weChishanu (Johann of Friday). Some people were saying the Tokoloshi is the one that killed all these people and it drank their blood as revenge for this dumping ceremony. In our culture they are thought, said to do so, especially for killing their benefactors. No one knows for sure whether the Tokoloshi left.

The biggest part of my mind screams, NO, to all these explanations. Yes there might be this ceremony, yes there was the N'anga, yes a lot of it is correct traditionally, but I can't seem to bite all these ideas. There has to be a bomb involved, somehow. The police and bomb experts are with me on this. They believe there was an incendiary bomb which would explain the noise destructions and the burns. The question is who planted it, and why set it to explode the same time this N'anga was doing his ceremony. Was this bomb also targeted at this businessman or the N'anga, or even owners of this place? But for whatever reason. There are a lot of questions that need answering

I am told they finally took the corpses (I mean the pieces, for I am not sure if they identified every piece and assigned each piece to its actual owner, since they were mixed up after the blast. What did the relatives of these people salvaged and buried? Did they bury their relatives, or a bit of each of the other 4 dead) to the mortuary, a day after it had happened. A huge contingency of security establishment (police, riot police, army, CIO) guarded the place and are still guarding the place as it swells with people coming from all over the country, coming to see number 4 Ndororo Street. It's a national security issue I suppose, especially with the issue of the bomb being the real deal, thus I suppose that's why the national security agents are also there. I haven't been there, and I still don't want to visit it.

It's now a mythical place for me. It is also a blood spot. I don't like seeing human blood, especially dead people's blood. The blood possesses me and I don't seem to know how to communicate with it. I remember some years ago (1999) when we were involved in an accident on our way to Botswana, on a trade endeavour there. We grinded down a small car under the bus we were travelling in, and the bus crashed the driver of this car into mincemeat. I had to watch as the police collected this mincemeat into plastic bag, whilst trying to prise the car from under the bus, and blood oozing out. It took me many years to deal with that. The picture is still there but now it doesn't possess me, obsessing me as it used to do. I didn't want to create another one by visiting this place of bloodbath at 4 Ndororo Street. Someday I will come close to it, but not now. I will stubbornly refuse its enticements. I will write this from some distance

Like I said, Chitungwiza is abuzz with conspiracies, gossips, plots…, just now I heard a huge snake was found in a taxi at the local bus stop as people abandoned it on the road, fleeing away from this snake. Is this snake another Tokoloshi? The taxi operators, like the above businessman, are known to have Tokoloshis in the form of snakes. Is this another Tokoloshi or it's just a ruse, or maybe just a lost snake that found its way accidentally into this vehicle.

Some NGOs, including the local council people were cleaning and clearing up the place, 4 Ndororo Street yesterday, removing the rubble, pitching tents, feeding people who were affected. I hope someone would help them reconstruct their homes and lives. The most disturbing effects of this is that the nearby children, from properties around this place, feel haunted, needed help to deal with the effects of this happening. The children are said to be afraid of getting outside their houses and play. This is one of the far reaching effects of such a thing. It might be what I am avoiding as well by refusing to visit this place. It will colonise me like it has done to these kids. It will take years and years before they do away with it. I hope there is some psychologist who will help these kids or the most affected to deal with this.

Friday 25 January 2013

I had a heart wrenching dream last night. I was dreaming we were going to an activity at the church youth group level. At one time I was saying I don't have money and won't be going but still I couldn't stop going. I kept going. She followed me. I am talking of Colleen, somehow she wasn't sure where I stood with her, so she kept coming, even though she didn't want to- and then I entered the event area, an enclosure, off a water point. It wasn't an intimidating water point, for there were lots of sands, and shallow waters. I kept getting in and I was almost there when I decided to check where she was. She was saying goodbye to a friend. She couldn't proceed in, she didn't have the license to keep following me in. and then she started retracing her footsteps back. She was so dejected, so lonely, so defeated, so desolate... My heart churned for her, clanged like a lonesome bell. I couldn't take it anymore so I started running out of this place for her. I felt I had to be with her and then I woke up. I felt gutted, so gutted with emotions and feeling. It took me some time for me to deal with this dream and the feelings it brought to me. I didn't even know if the dream had continued whether I was going to catch up with her and soften the pain, and tell her how much I loved her. Was she going to understand me this time?

*****

After digesting it for some time I realise I have to be open for her. I have to be patient with her. I have to wait for her, just a bit. And if she reaches out, I have to embrace her. I had been thinking of moving on to another girl but I think I need to wait a bit. It's my heart that is telling me to do so, or maybe I am doing that thing again, of trying to construct that which my psyche knows is not there so that I could deal well with the fact or the place that it should be.

*****

I think I had a terrible day today. There is this too self-important person I tried to get into contact with over payments, outstanding since last November, of my novel I sold to him (Keys in the River), who is also a church mate and I have known him for years and years. He has always looked down on me, self-importantly. I could have worked into a rivalry of some sort with him but I always shy away from it. There is a time, years ago when we liked the same girl and we jostled against each other in trying to win her. The girl liked me and I got her and he never liked it. But since we have been around each other for years we grew to respect each other, I don't know any other term to use here. He bought my novel, he wanted to read me. Today I had to wait for him for over 2 hrs in Harare city centre, and he still couldn't call to let me know what was holding him up. My phone had no airtime, I was broke… I only had bus fare back to Chitungwiza so I went to my former workplace, Amtec Motors in 4th street to borrow airtime from my former boss, only to call him and he now wanted me to take a taxi to his home, in the outskirts Avenue area of Harare city centre. I didn't have the money and the energy to keep chasing him through Harare. I think it was just a game with him, like I was his playing with monkey, laughing at me. I told him, brutally, to keep the money. I am no longer interested in the money, for I have wasted a lot in trying to get it. If I take the money he will be paying me for the expenses of trying to get it and my wasted time, not for the work, the tears, and the sweat I poured in creating the book. It seems he thinks he is so important and everyone has to run around for him, and everyone else's jobs, careers and homes, or even lives are not as important as his. I have had enough of his buffoonery, self-important attitude with me, so I told him to keep it.

Tuesday 12 February 2013

It's a long leap into the month of February without writing anything. I am stunted. I am bored, frustrated, just submerged. I need a breakthrough. Colleen is making my life a hell hole. I need a prayer and a wingman to get through to her. I am at the end of my tether.

Wednesday 20 February 2013

It has been an emotional roller coaster for me for the last 3 months, trying to deal with my feelings for her. I am done with her but there is still a lot of soul searching, the mind, heart, soul. We always try to figure out where it went wrong. There is realisation in me that I have lost out on her. Funnily, not to anyone this time around, for she says she is still single. She doesn't want to be with me, period. It has to do with me, its fine. I am cool with all this. I know I can get rejected, and I will take it well. There is cutting, a necessary tearing in me, but I will connect the pieces, eventually. I will be fine.

*****

I haven't been focusing well on my work for some time. I think for 2 weeks or so. Before that I completed a long short story of plus 6 000 words, WHEN HE WAS STILL CLOSER HOME, inside a week. It's a memoir story of my earliest life until when I was about 7. I can't say I completed it, for I want to continue writing it in another time, but I think I have enough for it to stand as a story of its own now. I am writing again, mostly poetry around the collection, A PORTRAIT OF. Last year I didn't write more than 5 poems for the entire year, didn't do much diarising for it was my off-year. I didn't place much poetry into journals and lit places too. I have been doing that for 4 days now, with overwhelming responses and acceptances, so I am a bit excited.

*****

My heart says yes, it is a yes. When it says saying no... it should be a no. I am trying to defy it, a bit this time. It doesn't give me much leeway. Maybe it's my mind that does that to me, I don't know how to separate each, sometimes.

*****

Its midday and it is so hot. If there was no clarity in my thoughts, today should have been a miserable day for me. I have just been working on some poems; I did 3 poems today, so altogether I have tallied over 16 poems for the past week or so. It means it's becoming a sizable or significant work. Another collection I have been working on is this diary collection. I have to decide on the titled between COLLECTING (GATHERING) EVIDENCE. But I have been accumulating the dairies, over 20 now. Another collection is that of short stories around the idea I have been toying around on for some time, even in the poems, dairies etc...., it's about finding one's path to home, so this story collection is entitled FINDING A WAY HOME (I think I have about 15 000 words altogether now). A collection of essays on language, art, thought and existence aptly entitled, LANGUAGE, ART, THOUGHT AND EXISTENCE is another collection I am working on. It's more like a writer's journey around these issues, not necessarily an academic take of it; a journey through life, a journey into places, into worlds, into ideas. These are the 4 works I have settled into working on this year. My intention is to have them completed by end of year, a tall order. It means when things get hire wire in relationship terms, I can always nudge myself back to reality by focusing on any one of these. There are other works I am working on, already completed but just needing a nudge here and there, a diary collection, IT'S NOT ABOUT ME (2010-2011 dairies) that I am typing slowly, and RAGE OF DEVILS, a play that needs a lot of working on. I will try to put in some work onto these too. I am also into a lot of photography but it's still for the love of it.

15

Running Away from the Lotus Position

I am running harder and harder, it's a cliff I am ascending. It is a very long cliff. The way down from this cliff has been enjoyable. I didn't have to put a lot of effort. It's always easy to say you are going running, long distance running. The school, Marist Nyanga, where I am an A level student, is just below the Nyanga range of mountains, so that running back to this school is running up the cliff. That's the hardest part of this long distance running for me. Twenty years later, I am on the floor, hard on my bum. I am in a lotus position. My knees are like corkscrews, the soles of both feet point, roughly, to the skies, giving thanks to the powers above. I am saying a mantra in Sanskrit, *Om mani padmi hum*. Why don't I say it in English or Shona? *Om mani padmi hum*, are there no Shona translations for this? For goodness sake we are in Zimbabwe, not India. I don't even know what they mean.

In the lotus position, I am reminded of twenty years ago. Running was something that was cool with my gang then, the school-going chums. Lotus is what is cool with my midlife chums, and that's why I am trying to find my position. Back then, even when I was running 6 plus miles from the school down to the junction on Nyanga road, and back to the school, I didn't still like it. But I was trying to create community with the cool kids. I never liked running, in general. Why bother. I would never be an accomplished runner like Tendai Chimusasa, Abel Chimukoko, Haile Gebre Selassie…no, I will never. But, I would still do it during every sports hour. I was doing this, I had been told, to gain fitness, physical fitness.

Now, I am doing this lotus to gain wisdom. Who said you have to turn yourself into a plant, or into a plant's posture to be wise. Are plants any wiser than us? The instructor told me wisdom comes from making the mind totally blank. Do plants have blank minds? Isn't a dead person supposed to be blank minded? Free from what, I asked her. From intrusive thoughts, unmuddied by flash floods of emotions, she said. But I didn't know how I could empty my mind. I suppose I could empty it the way we empty our bins on Tuesdays. But, it is the smell that stays, and a hallow place where the dirty was. Is that empty? *Om mani padmi hum*, is it the same as *hiha, hiha, hiha*, punting out steam, dirty, shit... My body glistens in sweat. I can barely hold my breath, only emptying it out concurrently with the, *ha*, in *hiha* chants. Every muscle in my body is stretched.

I was told that after every run, when the body has cooled down, I would find peace, relaxation, improved digestion, and a joyous merging of the cosmic energies in me. *Om mani padmi hum*, the instructor is telling me the same now. The extra benefits, she says, is it would cure my backaches, and any other aches. *Om mani padmi hum*, but it is creating some new aches, all over my body, my knees and feet are full of tremors, of aches. My being is becoming blank, my mind must becoming blank. My feelings are on the lower simmer, the floor is harder and harder on my bum.

It starts with believing. When you believe in it, you don't think of anything else, thus you get into this blank world. So, I tell myself- I believe I could reach peace of mind. I have the very best of instructors, a black belt welding instructor, a Zen roshi. Rice? It reminds me of rice fields in the south East Asian' sweltering, waterlogged lands, but this Roshi is an African princess. She is powerful and she carries a bamboo stick, and walks around softly- like a cougar. *Om mani padmi hum, hiha, hiha, hiha.*

I remember, one of my lower secondary school teachers, Nyamavhuvhu. He was also our sports master. He was a cruel lion. He was a bastard of the first order. He carried the unfurled, pointed thorny part of a strong fibre stem, behind us when we were running. If you were to be caught by him, he would bore your bum with this strong thorn, and it would pain like hell. My bum feels like that now. The floor is harder into me like those fibre thorns of Nyamavhuvhu. But you would cry out in pain, back then, and bolt at a high speed, away from, WHACK!, the bamboo stick. It hits me on my back. I blink harder, shake my head, and then try to concentrate on the lotus, on my mind. *Om mani padmi hum.* The bamboo stick, just like the thorn fibre, has prevented me from backsliding.

I am chanting, *Om mani padmi hum, Om mani padmi hum, Om mani padmi hum,* fervently. Why am I bothering taking this run, this lotus position? Ideas, intrusive, start spinning in me like Catherine's wheels. Who has said the body has to be exercised? Who said the mind should be exercised? Why? I can barely raise my legs- but I am still a kilometre away from the school. I could just let it go, walk a bit, cool down. My heart is on fire- I feel blood in my nose, in my head. My mind seems mixed up with hot blood, broiling steaming-hot water, it is a burning mind. I have since stopped the *hiha, hiha, hiha* chants, as I climbed the foothill, Mount Love. I don't have extra energy for that, anymore. The gravel road makes it so difficult for my footing. The road is too heavy.

Imagine yourself. There you are, a simple peasant, seeking enlightenment. After a barefoot walk across the foothills of the Himalayas, in the snow, you arrive at the appointed (who appointed it?) Bo tree. You are the Buddha, in a session now.

So that, after three hours of it, you open up your blank mind, and then you clear your throat- nothing is quiet. Birds are all over exploding in song, in the trees, the caw and roar of the bears, the wind whistling... This isn't quietness, WHACK!

Om mani padmi hum, Om mani padmi hum, I am trying again. *Hiha, hiha, hiha,* I have found my voice again. I have cleared away Mount Love, but it is still steep running. I am urging towards school. I know I would make it. It is just three hundred metres away. I know I would just bowl over in the grass, by the dorms, cool off a bit, get a nice drink, sip it with other cool kids, and talk about the run as if I had accomplished something worth the chatter. What?

Then, I would have my bath, and then go for the evening studies. It's just 45 minutes of evening study, but I hate it. It is so taxing to get through that, because one is anxious to discover what's beyond that. It would be supper, at six. Today it's a Friday, so it is my favourite dish- Sadza and chicken. The other days, it's always Sadza with beans, milk, beef, or worse with plain vegetables. My mouth waters, WHACK!

Om mani padmi hum, thank you Master, Mistress, I don't remember. But we are supposed to thank them for every bamboo connection with our flesh. There is no easy walk to enlightenment. My mind is full of pain. It is not blank, it is not blank, but it is now wiser. Doesn't pain and chaos make the mind wiser? It is the pain of hunger that has consumed me. I look around the room. All the other meditators are sitting in a lotus position, eyes closed. I suppose, their minds are full of nothing. Mine is full of hungry pains. I can't concentrate when I am hungry. I would stop doing any work when I was hungry. I would stop ploughing the fields. I would unyoke the cattle, and sleep off, or meditate the hunger off. Until someone who is cooking our meals comes with something to eat, I wouldn't wake up from this sleep. I would be so angry, so miserable, my mind so full of hunger. Nobody would talk to me. I would beat them if they tried. I would concentrate on my mind.

Now, I am older, I know what to do. You learn how to channel the hunger and anger with age, to make decisions without always resorting to violence and brinkmanship. The Roshi is gazing out the window, *Om mani padmi hum*. My back is sore, my bum is numb, my feet are upsides down, and my entire mind is burning in hunger. I am still running harder, though. There is only some fifty metres to the grass, but it seems the longest fifty metres, I have ever run. Inch by inch, millimetre by millimetre, I am crawling, in my lotus position towards the door. *Om mani padmi hum*, must mean, running away from the lotus position. What else would it mean? Nobody is noticing me, not even the Roshi, who is absorbed with the outsides. Inch by inch, I am getting there…, everything is darker and darker. My head is a cauldron of dark hot energy, and my chest is a blast furnace. Will I ever feel my knees again, my back, my feet?

I am still crawling in my lotus position. I hit the steps on the doors, and just tumble onto the walking path outside. There is screeching, whistling, and beeping of car horns, the steady hum of people passing by. I have unscrewed myself from the lotus position. I am up and bolting away as the Roshi's bamboo stick tries to connect. I am running harder even as I pain, like hell. My friends are off at the chicken place, I know. I am off to the corner of George Silunduka and Innez Terrence Street. There is a big chicken place there.

A moment later, here I am in the Chicken Inn, on my chicken-eating position, consuming a chicken burger with chips and coke. We are talking with my friends about the 6 mile run. Running from what? The lotus position? The chicken burger is really good. *Om mani padmi hum.* The chicken is good *hahi*, no, its *hiha, hiha, hiha.* Who cares, really? The coke and chips are heavenly, *Om mani padmi hum*, the Sadza is so filling, *hiha, hiha, hiha.* Wisdom must come with food.

16

The Evidence of Things Said: Dairies (2014-2015)

Monday, December 1, 2014

PHEW!!! I don't even know where to start with these dairies, what they will be addressing, why I should write them, keep them, what path they would take, why continue with diarizing when in the last dairies I could not do a lot of these, got bored, stopped altogether way before the endpoint of my dairy series. I have toyed with titles and have returned often to one title, but I don't even know why that title and whether I should take it as the title of these diaries. The last dairies I wanted to toy with the title- *Gathering Evidence*, but I still feel I didn't do well by it. This cycle will toy around THE EVIDENCE OF THINGS SAID, or is it unsaid, and it's obvious unsaid is the best title, because by writing them then I am saying those things unsaid. But I want to work with those that were said to highlight those unsaid, that's why I decided on THE EVIDENCE OF THINGS SAID as the title. Said and unsaid, I feel are shifting states of expression for each might work with the other, or precipitates into the each other. I tank it. But it's very clear I am still interested in evidence…, I still don't know what evidence, though!

******

Today is a cloudy, cool day (these are facts, evidence of this day) it seems the clouds are full of rains but it hasn't been letting out rains for days. It has been hot the last two weeks and now it has cooled down. I need the rains. By now I think you all know I love rain. I want it so bad that it rains. But it seems it has been raining up there in the clouds without a drop sneaking past the clouds to cool me down

******

I am listening to Enya's music on the album, Paint the Sky with Stars, beautiful music…that's not even the term for it, man. This is music, music, and music…too good to be described with words. I feel like if I could just ask me to help her paint the sky with stars I will never be able to stop myself from doing that for the rest of my life. I tend to listen to her music to cool down, especially when I am high-strung, too busy, too stressed, too impatient, feeling too good…and it softens all these down, and soften my insides, too

******

Am I in love, hahahaha, that perennial situation is with me? I am always thinking I am in love…but why. I don't know. Do I want to be in love, maybe it's a constant thing with me. I am always thinking I am starting out something with someone, holding onto someone, but it never really stays. I am writing poetry, stories, tales, plays, essays, novels, writing, writing, always writing. Sometimes I feel overwhelmed in the words I have put pen to. Are these my thoughts, what is me in these words. If they are all really me, then what's me now left secret, to me, something I haven't shared with anyone. A person can have all these words, these thoughts, send them out there into the world, my oh my I sometimes feel like just stopping this bleeding, clamming up and do something else, be somewhere else. Sometimes I wish I was an accountant, a mathematician, a statistician, I didn't have to use words. I don't have to leave behind a part of me that someone out into the future will read and call that me. 1+1=2, and it will remain like that and it would never belong to the statistician, accountant or mathematician, but these words, these thoughts will always belong to me, will shape into what the future will judge me for, will know me by. Being somewhere is what I really want to do. I have stayed here for far too long now. Never thought I will be around here longer than I have been. I want out now, so badly. I have tried to leave before but I didn't have enough conviction to do so. Now I think I really want out of this bloody hell hole. I said I have been writing too many words, and to stop doing that I have tried other art fields- photography which I started being serious about somewhere last year. And I have been publishing a lot of photography this year. I did start doing music and sound art last year too, and I have been publishing a lot of that too, and working on some more compositions. I want to learn some instruments, compose on these instruments, like the mbira, violin, viola, cello, and guitar...those are my favourite instruments. About midyear I started drawing too, and I have been drawing. Lately I have started on collagen and poetry translations, which I will be exploring too. I also do video work too but haven't focused on it that much. Thus I am panning out to be a multidisciplinary artist I have also thought I should be. My attitude about art is experimentation, collaboration (as the slim condition of possibility), being open to new things or to just newness, thus I will keep exploring all these art forms and fields more and more.

This year I have also completed my twentieth year as a writer, for I started in 1994, somewhere in the middle of that year , I don't remember the actual date in 1994, thus I have also been thinking of a retrospect of some sort, looking back to where I came from, going back there. Maybe I will create a complete works in one of the genres I started with in 1994, most likely poetry for I have been writing poetry constantly since 1994 and have in excess of 400 poems to date, which is significant.

******

2.59 pm. I have just had lunch- sadza with pumpkin leaves. Summer months I eat a lot of greens and summer weeds.

******

I am constantly planning on what I am working on. Checked whether there is anything more I can add to the novel, A DARK ENERGY. Yes the novel I have noted in my dairy circle, ITS NOT ABOUT ME (2010-2011), and I was writing it back then. Have since finished it and it has been with Zach Oliver's Aignos publishing co. Not a lot of progress about it for the past 2 years he has been with it. I was almost plucking it off his hands a couple of months ago, but I thought I should give him time, and I should have a look at it as he asked me to do again. There is not much change I can make to the storyline and narrative, but may change the presentation, and soften it a bit. Now I feel I can't do anything to it anymore, thus if he expresses reservations on it again, then I will pluck it off. It's frustrating me. I have been patient with him because we have worked well together on KEYS IN THE RIVER, when he was still the chief editor at Savant Books.

******

I wrote a poem in the morning whilst I was doing chores like watering the garden, cooking…, entitled *Body*. It's part of the collection I have just started, WHEN ESCAPE BECOMES THE ONLY LOVER, still at the legs level, but it will pan out into a huge book, I know.

******

I like this girl- incredibly *like* her. She is super-fun, confident, sweetly beautiful, and incredibly open. I can talk to her and forget where I am. I want to keep talking to her, fighting with her, agreeing and disagreeing with her, holding her in… my arms. I don't know why. She is going through a heartbreak, recently ended her relationship with her boyfriend. I am friends with both. She discovered a drawer-full of the boyfriend's dirty, which I knew though about, and hadn't told her. She is not really pleased with me now that I kept it away from her. I couldn't tell her all that. I don't tell. It's none of my business. I am glad she discovered that on her own and it's her decision to call off the relationship.

Wednesday 3 December 2014.

Yesterday I wanted to write something but failed, I had a hectic day. I am making last edits for my nonfiction book *Zimbabwe: The Urgency of Now*. I wrote it between January and April this year, and it's now coming out from Langaa RPCIG, my publisher of *Zimbabwe: The Blame Game*. The Urgency of Now is a follow up to The Blame Game…, focusing on Zimbabwe in the post power sharing period, the 2013 elections, and post these elections, too. It is a more focused

167

book as compared to The Blame Game, and bends more to the academic genre, the task of which has been trying for me, to follow academic rules. But I have to make an effort towards making it appeal to the academic establishment, which, even though The Blame Game was a bit unstructured, it has appealed to the academic establishment quiet well as it invades world-class University libraries and public libraries. So I will be focusing on this market with this new text. Most likely it will come out beginning of next year. I am a bit frustrated and strained.

*****

I am broke, but it's something I have always dealt with well. I know I will be okay, but still broke. Writing or maybe the arts is a thankless activity, but I hope someday I will get something out of it. Not that I write for the money. I will still write even if I am never going to get something substantial from it. Writing is breathing to me. I can't stop breathing.

It's sunny, hot summer day, and it didn't rain and the skies are now clear of clouds as if it never thought of crying, a couple of days ago. Why do I feel bereft and lost? I think it has always been a perpetual feeling with me. I don't feel I belong to anything, to anyone. Yes, I don't belong to anyone. I am lonely but busy, otherwise I was going to be more bereft and lost, frustrated. Does frustration act as my muse? I have often thought I write well when I am not frustrated. I don't know. Sometimes I do write well under frustration.

*****

I am drawing, writing poetry, stories, diaries, plays etc...., photographing things, making sound art, but why am I doing all these rather than to stick with writing alone. Why all this lot, yet I can't stop. It keeps me so much busy and away from my think-tank of a mind. Generally I am more fulfilled as an artist, even though as a person I am less so.

*****

Why is it that when one grows older they tend to feel a little more detached with everything, yet they should be a close feeling with things due to their familiarity. I feel I don't love, feel, have the same fouled up beautiful emotions and feelings over a lot of things. Some things or people I don't feel anything for yet I had felt so much more for, in the past. Where is that hot blood I used to have in my system? Have I been dying slowly, emotionally. I know physically I am dying slowly now, with my eyes on the forefront on this race to death, they don't see much anymore. It might be a very long road to the actual death. I want it long so that I might in the future find that feeling, hot feeling I had with things or some people. I know someone out there is telling me that there is no time, be whatever you want to be, feel those things now for you might die tomorrow. I know that. I don't care. But I also believe the hoping for something better in life, in tomorrow, drives us to keep trying, and one can do themselves a great hand if they believe there is always a chance, a hope for the best tomorrow. It is what drives us to keep trying, so I need this tomorrow, even though I know it's not guaranteed to me.

*****

I am angry with myself, or with some girls who make me angry with myself, especially when they say or show that they love me and yet I want to love them back and get the thing off, but I don't have it in me to do so. It makes me angry with myself. I know their love is inadequate for me. Most of these days I just ignore them; I need a stronger love. Something that would stop me, enslave me, halt me. I can't seem to find that love

Wednesday 10 December 2014.

I need to take time on these dairies. I have been incredibly too busy processing applications for university studies next year. I am focusing on getting a place next year in the UK or USA universities, and maybe do that masters in creative writing that I have vacillated on for years. I remember I first applied for this degree in 2009 at Hull University; got it but I couldn't take due to no finances for study. Up to now, I think I haven't taken it mostly due to failure of procuring funding. Even though deep down I also think this degree is of no use to me, I would take the chance given. This year I would try to look for financing seriously, or apply at universities that offer full funding like Iowa, Cornel, East Anglia

Saturday 13 December 2014.

I am not in a comfortable place with myself. I feel restless, baddish sort of, the energy around me is a bit dark, but I try to keep myself close to myself, not to overact at others. It has been a very funny summer so far. It is not raining. The skies, in the morning are always laden with heavy rainy clouds but it rains up there in the skies. Sometimes it's so cold you would almost think its winter, and then in the afternoons the skies clears up and it gets hotter. This year the change has been significant. I couldn't sleep well last night. This summer there are too many mosquitoes. They were all over me trying to bite me. I spent it trying to wade these off me; also there was just this restlessness around me. Maybe it has something to do with a girl I like who has not been behaving well towards me. I don't want to talk about her, until there is really something solid to talk about her. I am tired of these on and off girls, and my on and off into love life. Another thing I don't want to focus on these dairies is the political situation in Zimbabwe because of its on and offish way about them. It's like a soap opera, so I have tried not to follow it that much or write about it.

In short the MDC had its congress in October, and retained Tsvangirai on the helm, Douglas Mwonzora as the sec general. It's pretty much people loyal to Tsvangirai, people without open ambitions for his position who made the list, with rivals like Nelson Chamisa biting the dust. I think it's a let's wait and see leadership they created, maybe until we get to an election. There is nothing interesting to write home about this leadership in the MDC. Then the ZANU-PF had an explosive congress, last week. It started with Grace Mugabe's (Robert Mugabe's wife) bitchy (sorry for the use of this expression, but if it means something, then that's exactly how she behaved) confrontation, head on style when she lambasted everyone in the ZANU-PF who fought was against the president. She did it in a way never before seen or witnessed in Zimbabwe (even Mugabe lashing at Tsvangirai over the years was kid's stuff as compared to Grace's). She let rip and she focused the party towards where she wanted it to go (or where Robert Mugabe wanted it to go). In the process Grace got her PHD she never worked for at University of Zimbabwe, and the women affairs secretariat in the ZANU-PF. She made the party to push off most of its senior leaders (Mujuru in particular was stripped of her vice presidency by a colluding Mugabe), and others like Ray Kaukonde, Temba Mliswa, Didymus Mutasa, Jabulani Sibanda, Dzikamai Mavhaire, Nicholas Goche, Olivia Muchena, and the list is endless, lost their positions through this engineered push by Grace. Most of those involved in the wiki leaks debacle of a year or so ago were pushed, so it seems the machinery waited for an opportune time to deal with those and grace drives this machinery now. She aired, pointed, poked, raged, spat, like a crazy house wife every of these, especially the vice president, Mujuru. There were pushed out with the collusion and trickery use of Grace's by Mnangagwa's camp which now controls the ZANU-PF and Mnangagwa was given the vice president position he has coveted for years and is now the anointed successor of Mugabe. At least he is near Mugabe and can influence for successorship from close at hand but you can't rule out other eventualities in the ZANU-PF. It's possible to see Grace Mugabe adorning the winning jersey in 2018, but the most likely is we will have our old man in the wheelbarrow, being wheeled to the voting station, still competing for the leadership position in 2018, as long as he can still control his flock, which he has always been able to do, robotically. That's why I said the politics in Zimbabwe is boring because I don't even see ZANU-PF loosing 2018, not to Tsvangirai on his own, not to Mujuru on her own, not to the Lovemore Madhukus, Welshman Ncubes, Tendai Bitis, Simba Makonis of Zimbabwe, no...only, as I noted in *Zimbabwe: The Urgency of Now*, if all these were to unite into one opposition party, which I don't see them doing because these oppositions leaders are too egotistical, selfish and money-mongering idiots. So as long as Mugabe is there he will win it (whether through stealing or actually winning it by fair means) It is so tense, even a war is not just a far off thing. War is the only thing that can undo ZANU-PF. Grace broke the party down, but still it didn't die. The talk all over the country is now whether Mujuru is going to raise up and confront her humiliations or if she is going to fight quietly in the ZANU-PF, until she gets back into top leadership. Is she leaving the ZANU-PF to create a party of her own with the bulk of her followers and upenders noted above? Is she joining the opposition front with the MDCs. We can only speculate now.

■■■

17

Coldplay's X & Y, Angels, Him and Her

From the top of the first page
To the end of the last day

He has been through a lot.

He should just have given up, but he didn't. He still believed that someday, it would be fine. It's Ok now, and one can't expect much more than that. He is now in control, *going anywhere he wanna go?* One simply takes this Ok as the norm. One moves on with life, discovering it again. The Coldplay, in the song, *Square One* says, *The future's for discovering,* "....organ chords resonating in the spaces around Chris Martin's voice, insisting on churchly reverence to create sonic splendour. ....The music swells up with tremolo guitars, guitar riff raffs, strumming, chiming keyboards," *The Case Against Coldplay*

Richard Perry writes in *The New York Times Online, 5 June 2005*

The Coldplay band's music has been called "meditative" and "blue romantic"; it reflects on their emotions and Martin endlessly examines his feelings. Chris Martin's lyrical wordplay has been called feminist, and he calls the music, "limestone rock", which is the opposite of hard rock. Chris Martin is a great songwriter, but Guy Berryman, who is also the bassist, is even better than Martin.

"The music on X & Y can be considered to be thoughts and feelings of the Coldplay's doubts, fears, hopes, and loves." *Richard Perry, 2005*

But for him, there were those years of trying and trying…and he has nothing to show for it, other than scars. *Is he lost or incomplete? Does he feel like a puzzle, he can't find his missing piece?* He sings along to the Coldplay's song, *Talk*, "whilst a strummed acoustic guitar telegraphs aching sincerity", Chris Martin's sincerity, his own resonating sincerity, too, says *Richard Perry, 2005*.

The overarching melodies and guitar dynamics on this album are as imposing as Romanesque architecture, and then softly merging (like Byzantine Istanbul), solid and symmetrical. Their arrangements ascend and surge, measuring out the song's yearning and tension, cresting and easing back and then moving toward a chiming resolution. Its songs have been rigorously cleared of anything that distracts from the musical drama. *Richard Perry, 2005, Online*

Drama is what he knows. He has been through, one after another…, love dramas. So the music, with its non-drama like you would find, for instance, in Radiohead, he found his peace.

And there had been a parade of them; *talking in a language he didn't speak. And they were talking it to him.* The arrogant ones, the sweet ones who turned to poison, the egotistical ones, the angry ones, the bitter ones, the buffoons, the clinging, the bitches, the waifs, those who believed he would solve all their problems; the materialistic ones. The materialistic ones he understood. It's the society that shaped this want in them. Want for security, for socially accepted traits in a man, want to please the society. "I got one who provides", it is the chime song of these girls to their mothers. The problem was he couldn't provide for himself, let alone for anyone else. It was not about him leaving them, but more so, him not being strong enough, or at least strong enough in the other parties' eyes, to mean something socially acceptable in these relationships.

Maybe he had something to do with it, or was at a different place in his life... he tried to make them work, but they were just not happening. He had to deal with all that.

In him now, there is a little (lot) bit of all that, that they left him with. He doesn't know what he gave to each of these girls, in return. It must be something from each of these, being transferred around, like viruses. He is sick. He must be a really sick person. He is all these girls, yet he can't be all that, for he still believes in himself. With all that, he thinks if he was that, he could have given up on himself. Maybe, it is his point of strength; it was survival for him, to still believe he could be fine again. He believed it most when he could listen to Chris Martin, belting out, *The hardest part*.

The Hardest Part, it features a faster piano balladic sound, and starts with a repeating two-note piano riff, and features an instrumentation of a singsong guitar. It also includes a slow tempo with a drumming rhythm. The track ends with the band playing the repeated instrument riffs. *ImTheOnlyThugInTheBuildin, Sputnik Music blog, Online, March 12, 2013.*

It is his best song, of the entire album. It estimates, better than all the other songs on this album, what he had to go through. The band, Coldplay, helped him get through a lot of depression, despite many saying that Coldplay can induce it, that wasn't the case for him.

And the hardest part
Was letting go, not taking part
Was the hardest part
And the strangest thing
Was waiting for that bell to ring
It was the strangest start

So, it wasn't just one girl who did this to him. Maybe he did this to himself. He expected more from them. They always disappointed him, and it would cut into him. It is not fair for him to still blame one girl. But he can't help it. He had tried his *best, but didn't succeed,* with her. He had never been in love like that before; it is now nine years ago, when he fell for that girl. He had never believed in love at first sight until he met her. She was everything to him, and even now, there isn't a day gone by where he doesn't think "maybe this was the One for me".

They went out for 4 months, and they were amazing months, then he discovered she had another boyfriend. He became depressed because there was no other way of expressing how he felt. Despite all that, he kept opening himself in forgiveness, love and faith in her. He meant to make her his dreams. It was something wrong. And as what they always say when you love too much you get hurt very much. He loved and loved and loved, and all she could do was hurt him, terribly. *And the tears came streaming down his face.*

Especially, *when you love someone, but it goes to waste. He didn't know if it could be worse?* For some years, after he had realised that he was in that alone, he had drifted, into a square, *stuck in reverse.* It was *the spaces he travelled in,* square spaces, *waiting for the bell to ring.* In these square miles he was trying to break through. He would walk backwards on one side, hit the corner, then follow the other side, hit the next corner, and another and another. A square meeting more than four corners, it became a circle, a vicious circle. He couldn't push the sides of this square circle to create the make-believe music of a rectangle. *He climbed a ladder up to the sun. He could have written a song nobody has ever sung.* He had no song.

And he tried to sing. But he couldn't think of anything, really beautiful, Chris Martin doesn't sing the part, "really beautiful".

He was thirty, getting-to-thirty-one, guy. They got together for over three years, when he realised he was now all alone in it, and afterwards he had tried every possible way to bring her back to his life, for nearly two years, but he failed. He was so lonely.

She had been having an affair with another guy, all through the three years of their relationship. Despite her promises that she would cut it off, she couldn't, and then, he later discovered there were other men. She was a groupie...sex was an addiction for her, like drugs.

But, he could still seek love, ever afterwards. It was to find where to exorcise the pain. He met really good girls, but he couldn't keep them.

And the hardest part

Was letting go, not taking part, ...and to not take part in their lives, in her life anymore....maybe the bell to ring was more of a bell like in a wrestling match...he always knew things would end badly and no matter how wonderful it was, he found it strange that he was always waiting for the said 'bell to ring'. But in this wrestling match, the blows wouldn't stop, hammering him in the insides, even when he was the one throwing them at his opponents, those good girls later. It's him they were hitting.

He only wished she could have heard Chris Martin, singing that, *you really broke my heart.* That she broke his heart. She might have really understood what she did. *He had lost something he couldn't replace.* So that, he was broken inside; there was no space for these girls. He just carelessly let them go. And, once he had set on that, he didn't know how to stop. He let them go, one after another. *And he would get what he wanted, but not what he needed,* in them. *He felt so tired, yet he couldn't sleep.* They were not people; they were just crush dummies, he was experimenting with.

He drifted through, and there was another time he just let go. *It didn't matter who he was.* He lived in that world for a couple or so years. He never dated. Wondering *is there anybody out there who is lost and hurt and lonely, too.* He was in a foreign land, physically there, *bleeding all his colours into one? And if he came undone it was as if he had been run through some catapult it fired him.* Emotionally he was in a land full of strife, inside himself. *Wondering if his chance will ever come, he was stuck in Square One.* That land reminded him of those worlds in the bible when God had created the ocean, with waves furling all over, creating such massive tsunamis, typhoons, and hurricanes. He was looking for something more but he didn't know what it was. He was under this ocean, *trying to break through. Deciphering the codes in him, he needed a compass; drew himself a map,* to help him navigate through it all. Martin's voice and the lyrics softened it for him.

Martin places his melodies near the top of his range to sound more fragile, so the tunes straddle the break between his radiant tenor voice and his falsetto. You would almost think Martin is going to break...that feeling, in his heart....when it was too much, he felt he was about to break, but he stayed, so did Martin's voice. Martin can sound so sorry for himself, but he also found room in this to sympathise with himself. It doesn't matter he can't understand some metaphors Martin uses, it's the feelings they create, of standing together against all these difficulties of life before God has calmed everything. It was the environment in his insides, and somehow, he managed to keep his sanity.

If you can't think of something you could live for, think of something you would die for to live for, and it is something you could have. It's him he could die for. It's him he could have, he discovered. He dealt with the things, slowly, he did. Eventually he began to realise he was no longer numb with pain. It had been melting. He saw the land sprouting from the ocean, and the sun shining on that land. *He was now on the top, he couldn't get back.* He had to swim towards that land, s*eeing it in the new sun rising, seeing it break on his horizon.* He has been doing that. He doesn't want to go back to that world, again. He has learned his lessons well.

Some couple more years, he returned home. Yes, he was still hurt, but he could deal with it all without closing off. It had also made him stronger, he realised, fragile stronger. He was made human. Life can show people so much more. *He promised himself he would learn from his mistakes.* He came to an almost epiphany, that life really is so much more than personal gain, but for one to connect to all things.

But, he is more careful now. He has been in and out of it, but always staying out. He has been taking part in existence, in love, without getting into it. He knows this is not good for him. *He always feels like something's missing? Things he'll never understand. Little white shadows, sparkling and glistening.* He knows he needs to let go completely, and start having normal relationships. He knows he is now made up of the essences of good, and purity. He had just got lost, strayed off the path. If he can't now work to find the path, these distractions might take up all his life. His life will be a waste. But if he just listens to the voices deep inside him, he can almost always get back on track. He has to be part of the human race, *and all of the stars and the outer space. He has to become part of the system plan.*

The sun is there in the skies, the shadows are gone, only white shadows. *Little white shadows, blinking and missing them, he is now part of a system he is.* These white shadows resembles angels, subtle things like her, divine power. He knows if he gets to a really good girl he could let go, and become part of a larger system than *he is*. He has been thinking she is that girl. He calls her, "Angel". She calls him, "Dear". She makes him happy. When he is with her, he forgets all the other girls. He forgets they can be hurtful. He enjoys himself. It's when she is not with him when the *black shadows* return. *What if she is like all the other girls?* White Shadows vs. Black Shadows. *All this noise, Silence vs. Noise, he is waking up.* He is lost in thought, lonely, intuitive and afraid.

He knew her even before he had left home. She was young, 17, too young to really count. But he liked her. At one time, he almost told her he loved her. Now, he is not sure that was the right thing. He is glad he didn't. She would have died, the way those good girls who came after SHE had broken him, had died. All that lost goodness; it's not something easier to deal with. Now she is a big girl, beautiful, amazing. Her smile, you should see her smile. Such light shouting in joy from, it seems, coffers of light inside her. He spreads his energies into this unfolding morning light. She smiles as if he is safe. He wants to tell her not to smile at him, that way. He is not safe. He is diseased inside his heart. But, he can't. She is his angel. Angles have no choices, he tells himself. She has no choice, other than liking him. He wants to think she likes him.

He told her he likes her. And she talked to him as if it was a normal thing for him to like her. Generally she talks to him, and he would grow into the listening stance of a tree. Feeling like a boy, *he tries to listen to her.* It's the best he could do. He doesn't want to tell her that he is in love with her. He knows, *every step that he takes could be his biggest mistake. It could bend or it could break.* He is not sure, *that's the risk that he should take.*

He told all those girls he was in love with them. He doesn't understand the word anymore. What he feels for her can't be the same thing he felt for all those girls. For this one, it has ploughed deeper into his bones. He wants to tell her he has feelings for her, but he can't, as well. What would that mean to her? It doesn't really matter. He doesn't want to burden his angel. It's his woes he has to carry with him. She is happy, and he feels she should always be happy. He doesn't even know he can always make her happy.

There is a day, nine months ago, when he realised he had real feelings for her, or that he had started feeling things for her a long time before. He thought of himself as a collective soul of humanity, knowing that she is the girl he should have. Should, must…it didn't really matter because she was with someone. She still is with that guy, and he can't see himself winning her over. This guy, it's obvious, makes her happy. There was a talk at the church. Ten days, prayer days. He had been attending them, religiously, and that day it was questions and answers day. There was a fierce discussion, it was about whether Christians should visit and pay respects to fellow Christians who don't do the same for others when they face issues like illness, death etc.… *those who do not want to be part of a system plan*. She joined in the discussions, so confident in herself. It is what he admires a lot in her. She is confident. But that day, it was her voice that just whispered things into him. Her voice whispered to him, like the beautiful sounds of a gentle breeze, whispering to the leaves of the acacia trees, in the nearby forests. It still is her voice that makes him know that she is his angel. Voices like that belong to angels only, calming the world of chaos. After she had entered the discussions, the topic got closed. She decided it. She decided things in him, as well. She was the one. *Maybe he will eventually get what he wants. Maybe he is just stumbled upon it. Everything he ever wanted, in a permanent state.*

Nine months later he still can't tell her that, but he wishes he could just blurt out the things. *How can you know it if you don't even try?* Chris Martin asks him. He hasn't said anything even though, *an answer now is what he needs.* He knows if he is given a chance he can do great things with her. *Maybe he'll know when he finds her; maybe if he says it, he'll mean it. And when he finds her, he will keep her.* But she never asked for that in him, so he can't offer what's not wanted. He is taking what she is offering, friendship, and companionship and giving back what she is giving. *He is so scared about the future and he wanna talk to her, Oh he wanna talk to her,* but he can't.

Talk is built around a simple guitar lick (by Jonny Buckland.) (The track includes) a hypnotic pace, with (Will Champion adding) a metronomic beat to the drums.....” “The song features a synthesizer hook notable from Kraftwerk's “Computer Love”. It also adds a chiming note to more abrasive riffs during the breakdown near the end of the song. *ImTheOnlyThugInTheBuildin, 2013*

Throughout the song you feel like you are talking, eventually talking to that someone. But she is not telling him, talking to him, that he is right or wrong in loving her, but he doesn't towards her to this, as well. *What if you should decide that you don't want me there by your side?* Having something that is important to you means you have the risk of losing it, the Coldplay might be saying this, he thinks. It makes him worry, that maybe someday, she'll leave him... and that he'll realise he had all along been wrong. That he was the only one who was in this love. He is constantly scared he is losing people, and lately it feels like he has lost a lot of people.

He has someone who listens to him now. *You just want somebody listening to what you say. It doesn't matter who you are.* Yet

Coldplay also says, *but if you never try you'll never know, just what you're worth. Lights will guide you home and ignite your bones.*

And I will try to fix you.

Fix you, features an organ and piano sound. The song starts with a hushed electric organ ballad, including Martin's falsetto. The song then builds with both an acoustic guitar and piano sound. The sound then shifts with a plaintive three-note guitar line, ringing through a bringing rhythm upbeat tempo. Its instrumentation is varied with the sound of church-style organs hovering throughout the background, piano notes, acoustic and electric guitar riffs, drums, and a singalong chorus. *ImTheOnlyThugInTheBuildin, 2013*

Fix you is the best instrumental song on the album and manages to create a real sense of longing and sadness with some beautifully composed piano work in the background. Overall, it's his second best song, behind, *The hardest part.*

Generally, the lyrics on X & Y tends to focus significantly around the idea that everything is fragile, broken, out of place or missing; this is in almost all the lyrics of the album's songs, most notably in Fix you, *When you lose something you can't replace* and also in the song X&Y, *When something is broken, and you try to fix it, trying to repair it, any way you can* and Talk, *Are you lost or incomplete? Do you feel like a puzzle, you can't find your missing piece?* This theme is also reflective of the random, incomprehensible pattern on the album's cover (until you "fix" it using the Baudot Code).

But he wants to protest heavily against the Coldplay. He wants to tell them that there are wrong. Nobody can fix anyone. If you've ever 'loved' a BPD (bipolar disorder), or a drug addict, or even a groupie and sought to 'fix' him or her, you'll recognise the sadness when you finally admit to yourself that it's something they can't just help being and something you can't change. No matter what you do, you cannot 'fix' him or her…indeed; they will resent you for even having tried that. Some things in life just have to be accepted as they are: you must admit your limitations and move on, knowing they have a tragic future ahead of them and will have such a destructive impact on all those they have, and will meet. You only hope they remain oblivious to the harm they will do (especially to their children). If they would know, it would destroy them, all the more.

The image of the Baudot code fascinates him, though, which is visualised through a combination of colours and blocks, as a graphical representation of the Baudot code.

It is an early form of telegraphic communication using a series of ones and zeros to communicate. The code was developed by Frenchman Émile Baudot in the 1870s, and was a widely used method of terrestrial and telegraphic communication. To create the code on the cover of the album the Coldplay created coloured blocks, which are arranged in columns. In the left hand column the black and grey colours are one block, the blank space below it is one block, and the red/orange, orange/green and green/blue combinations below are each one block. A coloured block represents a 1 in the binary code and a blank block is a 0. Reading down, the code in the first column is 10111 which represents the letter 'X.' The far right column reads 10101, the code for the letter 'Y.' The columns in the middle, the blank space, represent the & portion of the album title. The Baudot code assigns five "bits" for each letter of the alphabet, an arrangement of ones and zeroes ("11000" is A, "10011" is B, etc.), as well as coding for numbers and symbols, like question marks or commas. To differentiate between numbers and letters, Baudot further broke the code down into "upshifted" and "downshifted" sections. Switching from numbers to letters — downshifting — would be identified by inserting "11011" into a message stream. *James Montgomery, MTV, 6 August 2005, Online.*

Code to centre, like an image of a meditating thing, it is this code, one has to discover, to be able to fix oneself. It should happen in the inside, communicating inside oneself…using one's own codes, to find their way again.

From the start in your own way. Maybe it's *Fix you's* compassionate, empathetic, magnanimous, inspirational feeling that gives you the feeling that you could fix somebody, fix yourself.

It doesn't matter who you are.

You just have to keep travelling on your road to some kind of safety. He is now travelling in his road. Maybe someday he will be able to fix himself. Maybe, some day, *darkness will turn into light.* Maybe someday his Baudot code will fix him.

18

A Date with Jonathon Matimba: An Appreciation of the Legendary Zimbabwean Sculptor

It was about seven, in the evening, when he arrived at our rural home, in Mapfurira village, Nyatate, Nyanga district, in the eastern highlands, Zimbabwe. He came with untie Linah, and my second cousin, Tatenda, his own niece. Jonathon Matimba, I have known him for all my life. He stays about 100 metres from this rural home of ours, still in Mapfurira village, so I grew up knowing him, but I knew him, mostly, as an uncle. There was good reason for him to come over to our place unannounced. He is a relative. He was coming to see me, his son, and I was with my brother's wife, Gamuchirai, visiting my parents.

I had arrived home the previous day, 18 June 2013. I never thought I could be writing much about this excursion home, for I was taking it as an opportunity to cool off a bit, to forget about the hustle and bustle of living, of trying to make a career in the harsh city of Chitungwiza. So, I left him alone as he talked to my father, my mother was talking to untie Linah, my mother's older blood-sister. I could only answer one or two questions directed at me.

It was almost when we were about to have our dinner when Uncle Jonathon started focusing on me. He asked me how I was doing. I answered him politely, "I am doing fine, Uncle". It was a guarded reply. So he said, "Come nearer, Tendai....., there is something I want to know". He speaks in a very low, soft, husky, gruffly voice as if he is running on low batteries, so I pushed towards him. We were sited on cement benches that covered two sides of the kitchen. Pointedly, as matter of fact, he said, "I heard you are now a writer". And I said, "Yes, I am, Uncle". He asked me what I had written, and whilst I was telling him about, *Zimbabwe: The Blame Game*, my then latest non-fiction book, I remembered he was a notable sculptor, himself.

I drifted back to 1992. It was draught year...so the crops we had planted in late 1991 had since dried. We had a lot of time on our hands, but we played. I was waiting for my "O" level results. But uncle had work for us. He would come early in the morning, had an old beaten truck, and he would say, "Bernard and Tendai, hop in guys". We would do so, after all, he had the cousins we played with. So the bunch of us (me, Bernard, Fungai (his son), Crispen, Paddington etc....) would go to the Muchena Mountains, to unearth the stones for uncle's sculptures. We sometimes didn't like it, so we would evade him. But most of the times, I enjoyed it. He is a great storyteller...he would tell us of the liberation war. He called himself, John Cann. I haven't been able to figure out where that name came from. So we grew up calling him that, especially when, we were playing at imitating our elders, we would imitate how he would retell those war stories.

Instantly, I knew what I wanted to do, I would write about him. I would tell his story. It was obvious he wanted to explore that with me, I discovered. So we agreed to explore it. I had decided I wanted to write an appreciation or a biographical piece about him, so we agreed to have some talk about all that in the morrow day, at his home.

The morrow day, I couldn't make it to his place, as we were doing all sorts of chores at home. It was the next day, two days later, when I went to his place. And, after a wonderful, egg and baked potatoes breakfast from untie Linah, that's when we started to talk. I had decided it was easier to have an interview to get into the mind of this reclusive genius, who is also my uncle, thus my elder. I knew it was easier to ask him some difficult questions, I couldn't have asked, if it was just going to be a general talk. He says he is not reclusive. But he wouldn't fool me here. He sure is. I don't remember one friend of his. He was always alone. He preferred our company, other than company of people his age.

He started by talking of his latest project, his latest portfolio of work. It is a collection of pieces, mostly of the animal world versus the human world? He tells me he had created these pieces from Munhacha tree (Parinari curatellifolio), which he had uprooted from my family's plot. I knew this tree on a personal level, from early childhood memories. Once, during the liberation war years, we did sleep under this tree, hiding away from Ian Smith's Rhodesian forces. Many times, after the war, this tree had provided a steady supply of the sweet Nhacha fruits for us. So, I wasn't sure it was worth it. But straight away I realised that the tree wouldn't only stay in my own memories, but would ignite many more memories, through the crafts that had been curved from it.

He bored it in the middle, left two opposing parts connected below and above. One side of the part has a black, naked man curved in it, and he calls him, Dumisani.

On the other side there are engraves of a cheetah, an impala, and a baby elephant. Here is the story. He says one day, before he could even uproot the Munhacha tree, he dreamt of this story. Dumisani went hunting and he found and caught an impala which he took with him to the cave. He didn't enter the cave though. He just hangs the impala on the tree behind the cave, without realising that the cheetah was sleeping behind the tree. When he had rested a bit, he left his impala on this tree, and went hunting for some more game, in the forest. He caught a baby elephant, which he took back with him to the cave, and he hangs the baby elephant beside the impala, still unaware of the cheetah. So the cheetah, baby elephant and impala adorns the other side of the piece, and Dumisani slouches on the other side, and between them is the cave. The cave is that hallow part dug off the middle of the Munhacha tree trunk.

As night drew closer there are two possibilities that Dumisani- the hunter- and the sleeping cheetah would have to grapple with. When the cheetah wakes up, it would be hungry, and finding two favourite meals hanging on the tree. But it would have to fight Dumisani to eat these, even eating Dumisani. If it succeeds it would have to enter the cave to sleep off the night. Dumisani would have to either be lucky he would get his quarry before the sleeping cheetah wakes up, and leave for home, or enter the cave with his bounty. If he decides to sleep the night off in this cave, it would create battle lines as they fight (Dumisani and the cheetah) each other for the right to use this place. Jonathon explained it up to that point and left it out for his followers to interpret or speculate on what will happen. He doesn't even name his sculptures. Straight away, I knew I was dealing with an awesome storyteller. It's not surprising, for I also come from the same language group and cultural structure. Nights in Shona childhood homes were always of eating great traditional meals, and storytelling. Jonathon continues this legend in his sculptures. He says his stories might appear like fables but they come from dreams. He says he has to dream first, and then tell the story, later.

With the other parts of this Munhacha tree he created some more sculptures. There is another piece of a lion that has caught an impala, and the lion is on top of the impala. Then a gun toting hunter comes on the scene, he shoots both the lion and impala. Another piece is of an eagle that has caught a snake, and is flying off with it. He is interested in the fight between entities (animals versus animals or humans versus animals). There are very stark battle lines he draws between the opposing forces. I ask him, why? Where is the gun fascination coming from? He says from his military background. He says most of his sculptures nowadays are shaped from his experience in the military.

Then I remembered the last time I came into contact with his pieces. In December 2006 he had a portfolio of work, stone sculptures. They were disturbing, ominous, and dark. They were an owl, eagle….and I think it was that owl that disturbed me. It seemed to bore into me, and I didn't like it. I couldn't wait to get out of the room they were in. They were all sorts of other animals. It was a very strong collection. This latest portfolio, I find, is not as strong as that collection. Maybe his creating powers are waning. He is old, frail…and he has been ill.

Jonathon started sculpture in 1975, at Mariga's place with the legendary sculptor Joram Mariga, Joram's cousins, John and Bernard Takawira, and Bernard Manyandure. He left this Nyatate group as he joined the liberation war, fighting for the independence of his country, so that, most of his sculptures have been done after he had retired from the army, thus therefore; the fascination with war, strife, battle, fighting. His sculptures are darkly fascinating and borders on the limbo land, when night meets day, thus he merges reality and dreams. The dreams come complete, but when he is sculpting, the day (reality), infuses into these sculptures.

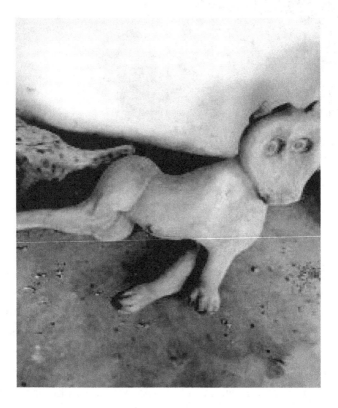

Even in the serene sculptures; of a sleeping lion, an innocent impala, the wild pig etc...., there is that dreamlike quality about them. In these sculptures he explores an opposite world to the world of fighting, gun toting, battle, strife. I feel it's a world he sometimes needs to enter. It is safe...and must represent that childhood home he grew up from, where things mostly existed for themselves. He even says he learned craft from young age when they would play at creating several different crafts in their younger playing days. I find the child in these serene crafts. It is his safety net, safety from the mad world of strife, fighting and gun toting. I ask him why sculpturing. He says sculpting opens up creativity than any other form of art. Does he believe in environmentalism? He says he believes in it, only as long as people are still allowed to hunt for certain specific, important reasons; like for regulated consumption purposes. "Not for the sport of it!" He says

He says pieces have been sold in the UK, US, South Africa. Some pieces are at the National Gallery of Zimbabwe, in Harare, some are at Nyanga craft centre, in Nyanga town. He also shows me business cards of important persons and collectors who have visited him, who includes Stephen Loitz (USA), director of US marketing and Shona Gallery, Dr Davidson Gomo, Super Mandiwanzira (Zimbabwean broadcaster now vying for the Nyanga South constituency, in the forthcoming elections). I am impressed.

Officially Jonathon is 73 years old but he puts his age between 78-80 years old. Back then, they would estimate their ages, for there was no proper registrations of births, most of which happened in people's home, not in hospitals. They would use events like when the locust drifted from the north, or when there was draught, etc...., so they were always rough estimates.

Jonathon works with both stone and wood, and he can work on both, at the same time. He doesn't have any preference between the two, only that when he dreams he is shown which to use as a vessel (stone or wood). So his dreams are very clear, thus he doesn't sculpt from reality's base. He feels reality can easily be copied. He can only work outside of dreams when he is trying to sculpt things not from his world, like a dolphin, but he uses a picture, which is an extension of a dream to him.

He uses different types of stones. He doesn't particularly like soapstone because it requires too much polishing. He doesn't like polishing for it represent artificiality to him. He gets his stones from around Nyatate, Nyautare to the north, and Muchena, in the mountains to the north. On wood, he prefers Munhacha tree, Blackwood (Mukodzi tree). He prefers to use softwood because greenwood sips and cracks, so would crack dry wood, too. He uses traditional tools to craft his pieces like the chisel, hammer, mbezo, and axe. He doesn't use sculpting machines that the new generations of sculptors are using.

Does he have a new dream? Yes! A couple of weeks ago, he tells me, he dreamt of a non-African animal…he says it is the Australian kangaroo, eating a snake. He says he has been obsessing about this dream, and he would like to tell it, some day very soon.

He tells me he was born to be a sculptor, but the circumstances forced him to forego a lifetime career of it, as he pursued a military career. Does he regret that considering that his contemporaries (Mariga, Takawiras, and Manyandure) became very important sculptors to ever come out of Africa? He feels fulfilled with his work in the army, his family, and his work now as a sculptor. They joke with untie Linah about this decision. Gamuchirai, my brother's wife asks untie, "'So, Untie, I heard you were the one who refused uncle to pursue a sculptor's career, after the war". "Yes, I did, daughter. I couldn't let him leave me again. It was difficult looking after the kids when he was in Mozambique, fighting the war. I couldn't allow him to leave me again." And Jonathon agrees, "Yes, your untie was afraid I would go to America, or Britain with this new career, so she said I should join the army, and stay home after the war, and I did that."

He has no regrets. He is happy with his choices; he smiles, as usual, a carefree smile. He feels complete. After finishing every dream piece, he says, he feels complete.

Jonathon doesn't drink, or smoke, likes vegetables and Sadza, dreams about battle lines between opposing entities in creating his darkly, complex, fascinating sculptures, in the little village of Mapfurira, alone. Yes, he is the only one left, for his contemporaries (Mariga, Takawiras, and Manyandure) are all gone. I ask him if he is reclusive. He says he is not. Why doesn't he work with others at Nyanga craft centre? He says he doesn't like to work in groups. He says dreams don't go with crowds. It is individual.

19

Music and Me

I would never become the greatest sing to ever come from Zimbabwe, Chitungwiza, and let alone Africa or the world, but I love music. I am crazy about music…any music. It plays well inside me than it would ever for some of Chitungwiza's musical greats. It's a crazy assertions, I suppose, considering that Chitungwiza is the capital city of Zimbabwe's music. All the most influential bands and musicians have come from Chitungwiza. It's a hot bed for artists, not just musicians, but theatre, dance, literature, sculpture etc.

I believe they might be better writers out there than those lauded. Whether they would ever get the space, or create the space to take their rightful place, I don't know. I don't mean generational, I mean in this space I inhabit, not write in. the same applies to my love of music, the music that really plays in me. I think of music not just in recorded music…there is recorded, written, and visualised music. Maybe the reason I can't seem to exhume it out of me is because it is out of my scope, is too large for me. I can't even say I am talented as a musician, but maybe that I am a talented listener. I feel it's an art, just like making music is an art, to be a talented listener. You need to have the ears, not just here and there on your head. In listening to music, you create the music with the singer or musician whilst the song is playing. That applies to books, visual art etc., the greater talent is on the reader, the consumer. The one who has ears or feelings or senses to understand the art offering. To understand the book better than the one who wrote it. I will be the first to admit there are readers out there who understand my work more than I do, or would ever do. My job as a writer is to be just a vessel in which the stories are exhumed from out of me, or not necessary out of me. Where the stories comes from is where the music comes from, or poetry, painting, drawings etc. Robert Duncan in his statement on poetics, *Disclosure*, believes poetry comes from God. He doesn't want to be praised as the one who created it.

There is no such a thing as a first-rate poet, and, because a poem is a service of the divine, I would maintain that there is no such thing as a first-rate poet... Likewise, wherever a man writes in the make of Poetry, he writes in the office of the Poet in order that there be a poem, and if he claim personal honour for the act he usurps the honour. *Robert Duncan, 1959, Eleven Journal, issue 15, 2013*

I find resonances with this thinking in assigning the work that I produce in creative writing to something else other than me. I can't conveniently say it comes from God but I am not also saying it doesn't come from God. If I say everything I write comes from God, I might have to be a religious writer or specifically a Christian writer since that's the God I know of, was taught and embraced. I will settle for it is informed by God, but I am not a religious writer. I am just a writer. In refusing ownership or assigning ownership to creativity, I might have to accept ownership to interpretation (listening). I listen better to music than to literature. This is where my greater talent lies. I can say; offer me any type of music, beat, and as long as it is well arranged, written or sung, I would love it. Even music that critics of music would tear to pieces, I listen to them better. I think it's the soul in me that makes them works of great beauty when a lot of people are trashing the same stuff. *Music is music*, to borrow from Bob Marley; it's the ears of the listeners where the beauty beholds the music, not in choices. It is in acceptance of beauty, whatever the beat, music, language, conventions, and traditions.

I see huge crowds of westerners listening and dancing to Thomas Mapfumo and Oliver Mtukudzi's traditional Zimbabwean mbira flavoured music, far away from the home of this music. It's this universality of music that makes it pervades all other things created by man, for man. It reaches where other art forms fail. If you write a book in Shona, someone who doesn't understand that language, unless it is translated, would never know or understand what you wrote about. Visual art has that universality, but music goes much further. With music you don't even need any translations; you don't need to see it. Listeners would love music even for its strangeness. It is the beat that it creates or builds, the love or liking of the beat and words, the feelings it invokes…. It is a universal language on its own.

There is this song I love from *Salif Keita,* titled *Mandjou.* I don't know what he is singing about. It's the feeling he sings the song with that makes me feel like I hear what he is saying, it's the beat, the sound, the total sound sphere it creates that makes it one of my favourite songs

Someone might cry over a song, a song that makes someone else laugh. Another might ponder, another might be angry with the same song. Unlike all the other arts, music just doesn't always accrue the same feelings from different people listening to that same song. The listeners take it inside themselves and it defines the world inside these listeners. It is not the singer who does that, it is the listeners who would do that to themselves. Books do that to a certain extent, but music goes further than books, in its individuality, in interpretations, in universality, in acceptance.

Even in books, other than the story plot, I am also touched by the musicality in words. It's the music in words that make writing much more interesting, not just words, even the musicality in the ideas the words bring out, the metaphors, the institutions…

I started listening to music, I would like to think, in my mother's womb. My mother loves singing and music and it must be where it came from. I knew of myself, as I remember now, I was always singing. I was in the school choir in grade 1, with a certain Mr. Mwedzi, at Nyatate primary school in 1980, and I used to do a great tenor in this choir. I remember it was the three of us from the same village; James Gwanyan'wanya the late Amon Mapfurira and me who were the main tenor voices of that choir. All through primary school I was in this choir.

Some year, I think it was in 1984. We were invited to the official opening of the adjacent Nyatate secondary school, our choir was going to sing at that ceremony. It was those years of boyhood mischievousness and I was full of that kind of shit. We sang our hearts out and my mother was so proud of me, until I made another of those trademark badass mischiefs of mine. When it was time for eating, the caterers gave us a big basket dish of sadza, and two small dishes of relish meat. The big notorious Nyatate secondary school boys grabbed these and made for the bushes and mountains nearby. I couldn't let them, me and a few other notorious little boys of Nyatate primary; defraud us of this food we had sung prettily for. It was supposed to be food for both choirs, primary and secondary, so we tailed these old secondary school boys into the bushes.

Mother later told me she was so ashamed seeing me running after these rowdy boys, but I got respect from these rowdy boys for not being afraid of them and for standing up for what was rightfully mine. We had a great feast of it, to quench the hunger of having belted our voices in a song. I love food, not just cooked food, just food. Music is like food to me. You need it every day to replenish your soul. I can spent a full day without doing anything worthwhile, without thinking anything huge, but I can't do without art, without music, without food. Days I manage to do so are horrible days for me. I am frustrated, angry, depleted, and empty. In days I would be dealing with stressful stuff, if I listen to a really good song, the stress loses its jagged edges. Food fills an empty hole in my soul that seems to be in my stomach. I try to keep good food by me so that I can always use it for this purpose, knowing it won't also be dangerous to my health. It is the same with music. There is nothing that beats listening to a really good song, or music.

References

Archuleta David, 2010, *All I want is you,*

Butler Judith, 2004, *Undoing Gender,* Routledge, New York

Chimamanda Adichie's, *The Danger of the Single Story,* Youtube.com, 7 October 2009,

Coldplay, 2005, *X&Y Album,* Capitol Records and Parlophone, London

Coolidge Clark, DuPlessis Rachel Blau, Palmer Michael, Yau John and Young Geoffrey (speech) 1985, *image and imaging 2,* Tyler school of Art, Philadelphia

De Gruchy John and De Gruchy Isobel, 2006, *The Volmoed Journey,* Volmoed, Hermanus

Duncan Robert, 1959, *Statement on Poetics: Disclosure,* Eleven Eleven Journal, issue 15, 2013, California College of Arts, Oakland

Hermanus and Volmoed tourist information can be accessed Online here.

Howe Susan (interviewer), Bernstein Charles and Andrews Bruce (speeches) March 14, 1979, *Language,* Pacifica Radio Poetry Show, New York

ImTheOnlyThugInTheBuildin, March 12, 2013. Sputnik Music blog, Online

Mitchell Francesca, *South African History,* Online, Public History Internship, Cape Town.

Montgomery James, 6 August 2005, MTV, Online.

Morris J, 2010, *Secret passageways/Nathaniel Hawthorne vs Bernadette Mayer,* Eleven Eleven Journal, issue 9, California College of Art, Oakland

Mwanaka Tendai, (unpublished novel) *A Dark Energy.*

Mwanaka Tendai, 2016, Playing to Love's Gallery, Royalty Publishing USA

Mwanaka Tendai, 2015, *Finding a Way Home*, Langaa RPCIG

Mwanaka Tendai, 2012, *Keys in the River*, Savant Books, Honolulu

Mwanaka Tendai, 2013, *Zimbabwe: The Blame Game*, Langaa RPCIG

Paiget J, 1968, *Six Psychological Studies*, translated by A. Tener, University of London press, London

Perry Richard, 5 June 2005, *The Case Against Coldplay*, The New York Times Online

Edward Sapir (1921), *Language: An Introduction to Study of Speech*, Harcourt, Brace and World, New York.

Soanes Catherine (ed), Hawker Sara (ed) and Elliott Julia (ed), 2001, *Paperback Oxford English Dictionary*, Oxford.

Stones E (1966) *An Introduction to Educational Psychology*, Methuen, London.

Veit-Wild Flora, 1992, *Introduction note to The Black Insider* by Dumbudzo Marechera, Baobab Books, Harare

Veit-Wild Flora, 2012, *Me and Dambudzo: a personal essay*, Online

Whorf Benjamin, Lee (1966) *Language, Thought and Reality*, MIT, Cambridge, Massachusetts.

Wilkinson Andrew, 1971, *The Foundations of Language: Talking and Reading in Young Children*, Oxford University Press, Oxford.

Printed in the United States
By Bookmasters